ALSO BY JANIS ALLEN

PERFORMANCE TEAMS:
Completing the Feedback Loop

I Saw What You Did & I Know Who You Are

I Saw
What You Did
& I Know
Who You Are

Bloopers, Blunders and Success Stories

---

on Giving and Receiving Recognition

JANIS ALLEN
with Gail Snyder

Published by Performance Management Publications
3531 Habersham at Northlake
Tucker, Georgia 30084
(404) 493-5080

This book was set in Garamond.

Administrative Editors: Brenda Jernigan, Sandy Stewart
Production Coordinators: Sandy Stewart, Tracy Quarles
Cover Designer: Billy Johnson
Printer: Tucker-Castleberry Printing

Library of Congress Catalog Card Number: 82-061868
International Standard Book Number: 0-937100-04-8
Printed in the United States of America
1 2 3 4 5 6 7 8 9 – 98 97 96

Dedicated to my parents, G. E. and Pauline Allen, who have given me my most important experiences with positive reinforcement from day one.

FOREWORD

Nothing is more important to a high performance organization than positive reinforcement. Nothing is more important to successful positive reinforcement than delivering it correctly—a skill in which Janis Allen excels.

In this book, Janis draws from 18 years of experience with implementing Performance Management systems in numerous U.S. businesses. The book is filled with real examples that illustrate the do's and don'ts of delivering reinforcement, examples that are often humorous, sometimes touching, but always memorable.

This book will certainly help readers enhance the effectiveness of their reinforcement and recognition, and, as such, increase their organizational effectiveness.

It's difficult to believe that over 20 years have passed since Performance Management was introduced as a systematic way of motivating employees. Yet, during that time, no book has been written on one of the most essential aspects of that system—the effective delivery of positive reinforcement. With this book, Janis Allen has fulfilled that need.

Aubrey C. Daniels, Ph.D.

PREFACE

Neil Biteler, a Performance Manager for AG Communication Systems says, "This technology is five miles deep and we've only got a spade."

Many people are rediscovering the reality that "the more you know about a subject, the less you know." This is especially true of human behavior. They're interested in fine-tuning the way they recognize and reinforce people. No longer are they satisfied with a recognition system that merely runs; they want a system that purrs. This book is for those people.

TO THE READER

My only fear in publishing this book is the reader's possible reaction to the large number of personal examples I have used. Because I mention reinforcers I have received and why I received them, I fear you will view this as bragging.

However, I'm going to close my eyes, brace myself, and use these examples anyway. Receiving positive reinforcement is a very personal thing. Only the person receiving it can determine what is reinforcing and what isn't. Therefore, the only reactions to attempted reinforcement that I can be sure of are my own. So, these are the ones that I have the most confidence in telling.

Please forgive me if I appear to blow my own horn. Even as I write, I realize I have more to learn about receiving positive recognition. Yet, I must confess, it does feel good to tell these stories.

Janis Allen

ACKNOWLEDGEMENTS

The following people took the time to read the draft of this book. They increased its value with their opinions, suggestions, and POSITIVE REINFORCEMENT.

Jim Audo, Walgreen's
Mary Bloomer, Kingsport School System
Ed Budd, Delta Faucet
Jim Carroll, Eastman Kodak
Byron Chandler, Aubrey Daniels & Associates, Inc.
Dean Crosswhite, Kingsport School System
Aubrey Daniels, Aubrey Daniels & Associates, Inc.
Jamie Daniels, Aubrey Daniels & Associates, Inc.
Ann Davis, Aubrey Daniels & Associates, Inc.
Vic Dingus, Tennessee Eastman
Mike Grant, Amoco Canada
John Hahn, Eastman Kodak
Al Hauck, Eastman Kodak
Brenda Jernigan, Aubrey Daniels & Associates, Inc.
Gayle Jones, Honeywell
Sue Jones, Blue Cross Blue Shield of Michigan
Bill Lilly, Eastman Kodak
Betty Loafmann, Aubrey Daniels & Associates, Inc.
Donna Martemucci, Eastman Kodak
Andy Morency, Aubrey Daniels & Associates, Inc.
Asa Moseley, Allied Systems
Katie Muldoon, Eastman Kodak
Elmano Nigri, Grupo Isaias Apolinario
Elton Apolinario Nigri (Kiko), Grupo Isaias Apolinario
John O'Connell, Aubrey Daniels & Associates, Inc.

Pete Pirri, DuPont
Jerry Pounds, Aubrey Daniels & Associates, Inc.
Nancy Scott, Eastman Kodak
Sandy Stewart, Aubrey Daniels & Associates, Inc.
Jim Smith, Eastman Kodak
Marie Wagner, Aubrey Daniels & Associates, Inc.
Steve Walker, Honeywell
Susan Webber, AG Communication Systems
Jack Weller, PPG Fiber Glass

Table Of Contents

III. When People Won't Take Your Recognition

IV. Receiving Recognition Gracefully

V. Putting It All Together

I.

Giving Quality Recognition

Positive Reinforcement
And Recognition

*T*HE FINDINGS SHARED IN THIS BOOK are based on 18 years of experience in discovering the most effective ways to give positive recognition to people in the work place. This has been done while helping organizations use the Performance Management system of dealing with people.

Briefly, Performance Management (PM) is a database system for managing human performance at work. With PM, we determine the results we want, pinpoint the behaviors which will accomplish those results, and use measurement and feedback to determine when to give positive reinforcement for improvement.

Positive reinforcement is the most crucial aspect of the system. It occurs when a person receives something he or she likes after accomplishing a specific behavior or result, and increases the likelihood that the behavior will occur again.

Developed by Dr. Aubrey C. Daniels, PM's roots and principles are those of Applied Behavior Analysis, the science of behavior originated by Dr. B. F. Skinner. Though all the components described above must be present for effective Performance Management, this book's purpose is to examine in-depth the keystone of the system: positive reinforcement.*

Let me talk about the difference between positive reinforcement and positive recognition and explain how those terms will be used here. According to Dr. Daniels, positive reinforcement is the consequence a person receives during or immediately after his or her behavior. This consequence increases the probability that this behavior will occur again. [Positive] recognition occurs sometime later — hours, days, weeks, or longer.

The word "recognition" is more common in our vernacular. Recognition itself is also more commonly used than positive reinforcement because of the difficulty in giving reinforcement while the behavior is occurring. Though positive reinforcement is certainly preferable, giving recognition is often the best we can do, because we weren't there to see the behavior occur. In this book, we explore how to get better at giving and receiving both.

*For more information on Performance Management, read Performance Management: Improving Quality Productivity through Positive Reinforcement by Aubrey C. Daniels, Ph.D.

Toward
Quality Recognition

OFTEN WHEN WE TRY TO GIVE RECOGNITION TO PEOPLE, we run into problems. Some of our best intended recognition efforts, unfortunately, work against us.

When we give recognition to groups of people, our recognition might be unfairly distributed to individuals. Since individuals in a group contribute at varying levels, the same recognition can be too much for the lower performers and too little for the higher performers.

And what about tangible forms of recognition — things that cost money? What standards apply in giving private versus public recognition? How can you help your co-workers, family and yourself become more self-reinforcing?

Telling someone, "I like what you did," is not a natu-
rally-occurring act for most of us. We expect a certain
level of performance from other people and have difficulty understanding when they don't do what they're
paid to do.

Today more companies provide recognition and ex-
posure to employees and teams at the conclusion of
long-term special projects. These attempts are com-
mendable. However, they do little to positively change
or improve performance. Unless positive reinforcement
for performance occurs frequently, it has little effect on
behavior.

We must work at our own ability to give deserved recognition, not just for "over and above" performance, but
for expected dependable and consistent performances
which keep our organizations running every day. It's so
easy to take good performers for granted, letting "no
news is good news" become our manner of operating.
Unfortunately, people around us then form the impression we do not value what they do. Taken to the extreme
they lose the food which is essential to their being. As
Dr. Jacqueline Damgaard, Atlanta clinical psychologist,
puts it, "Life can become meaningless when our behaviors don't seem to matter."

Most organizations have increased their attempts at
providing more recognition for individuals. Unfortunately, attempts at recognizing performance don't always have the effect on the receivers that we intend.

Recently, a New York publishing firm formed a committee to examine the organization's recognition sys-

tems. For years the company had sponsored an expensive and lengthy awards luncheon. At the luncheon, only a handful of employees received awards while the remainder served as audience. After the luncheon the entire staff could go home. When the committee opened the door to employee feedback, the widespread sentiment expressed was: "We don't want to go to a luncheon. Why don't you save the money and simply let us go home early?" Management got the message.

*L*ife *can become meaningless
when our behaviors don't seem to matter.*

Personalization

An INTENDED REINFORCER ISN'T A REINFORCER unless the recipient wants it. Remembering this will help you to reinforce in ways others like. It will also remind you not to overuse any particular reinforcers as people tire of anything that is used too frequently.

Tangibles such as company logo items often trigger tangible burn-out. Having dozens of key chains, coffee mugs, and caps printed and in hand makes it tempting for us to offer them at every opportunity. Novel and fun at first, they can quickly become boring even though we may want to scatter them around as advertising. Using only these items for recognition places too much emphasis on the company, and not enough on the person. Anything you buy by the gross probably won't be reinforcing for very long.

Some well-intentioned managers use group recognition exclusively. They find it easier to bring in a pizza for a dozen people than to go out and find different reinforcers for 12 individuals. People also tend to rely on tangibles (material items) because with tangibles it's clear in everybody's mind that something has been delivered. They can point to a visible object, anchor in on it, and say, "I gave them those T-shirts," or, "Remember when we had the pizza?"

The most memorable reinforcer is an individualized one. Giving group reinforcers or en masse celebrations are important first steps in your reinforcing efforts. Group reinforcers are valid attempts at recognition. They are, however, attempts which only scratch the surface of true quality recognition.

Anything you buy by the gross probably won't be reinforcing for very long.

Quality Recognition

So, WHAT IS QUALITY RECOGNITION? Many organizations, in their quality efforts these days, define quality as "meeting customer requirements." Applying this quality model to positive reinforcement, your "customer" is the person you are trying to recognize. It may be your co-worker, your manager, someone who reports to you, or someone at home. To make your reinforcement efforts successful, view the reinforcees as your customers. Determine what they want and what their requirements are for feeling reinforced. When you learn all these things and deliver them at the right time, for the right things, in the right way, and to the satisfaction of the recipient, you have learned the skill of quality recognition.

We must keep in mind that when it comes to reinforcing, there is a relationship between quantity and quality.

With reinforcement, quantity enhances quality. The more reinforcing you do, the better you become at it. Often, the people perceived as good reinforcers are simply those who reinforce often.

The more you reinforce, the more you will know what works and what doesn't work. You will become skilled at the craft of recognition and reinforcement. You will find who likes this and who doesn't like that. The more you practice, the more comfortable you will become at delivering positive reinforcement. The first pinpoint to quality recognition, then, is to do it often. Look for every opportunity.

*When it comes to reinforcement,
quantity begets quality.*

Toward Self-Reinforcement

*T*HE LONG-TERM GOAL FOR REINFORCING is to teach people how to become self-reinforcers. An organization's goal should be to teach employees how to recognize and take in the natural positive reinforcers they get when they help the organization. This doesn't give us the go-ahead to say, "You're supposed to reinforce yourself, so go out there and feel good about that job you're doing." We're not off the hook.

First, we show people how and why we value their work. After many experiences with this, they can become independently reinforcing. They remember our approval when they repeat the reinforced behaviors.

When you point out to the individual something about the way he does his job that is of genuine value to the organization or to you, you bring that person closer to self-reinforcement and to goal attainment. After all, everyone wants to feel that their contribution is important. We start knowing our contributions are important when other people tell us.

If you mention something to the individual about the preparation, the follow-through he did, or the extra care he took, you help him become aware of the specific behaviors which are desirable, that add value, and that you want him to repeat. Every time he faces the choice of repeating that behavior, he can replay that mental tape. Then, he will pair the reinforcement with whatever he did the last time.

That is what self-reinforcement is: When we've had enough reinforcement from external sources — other people whose opinions we value — we remember that good feeling and are likely to do the behavior again.

In my work with clients, someone invariably asks, "What about good old-fashioned self-motivation? You talk about patting people on the back and giving them positive reinforcement. What about those people who perform well and don't seem to need that much attention?"

It is easy for us to understand that we must first feed a child before he learns to feed himself or dress him before he learns to dress himself. The parent must initially do the tasks that eventually become routine behaviors when the child matures. The same is true of self-reinforcement. It isn't genetic; it's learned.

However, most people prefer to think that characteristics such as determination, assertiveness, and pride in a job well done, are innate properties. In reality, we learn the behaviors which manifest these characteristics. Self-motivation is learned. It comes from the consequences of our behaviors. We learn to be self-motivated, determined, and assertive in the same way we learn to feed and dress ourselves.

Many people, during their childhood and adult lives, haven't had much positive reinforcement. Their parents held back on praise, attention, and recognition, possibly thinking this would make their children self-reliant. It does the opposite.

A lack of reinforcement history often makes it very difficult for people to receive and give positive reinforcement. Yet, receiving reinforcement is a pre-requisite for becoming a self-reinforcing human being. The more positive reinforcement you've had in your past, the easier it is, at some point in your life, to be able to internalize it.

Sadly, some individuals learn at an early age to drive themselves and others by using only negative reinforcement. They perform only to avoid something negative, such as the disapproval of a parent or a boss. We use the tools that we've been given.

Even self-reinforcers run out of fuel without recognition for the value of their work. We have to fill their tanks full and keep them on the right road by letting them know our opinions on how they're traveling.

We need to learn how to make the most of naturally occurring reinforcers, such as the pride and intrinsic good feeling people get when they do something well.

Betty Shunk, a former boss of mine, helped me to become more self-reinforcing when I was new in my job as a consultant. She asked me to give her a list of all the things I'd been doing that I was proud of. She and I always traveled in different cities, so she was not in a position to observe my work.

I started my list sitting on a plane one day, and was surprised at how many items I came up with. I wrote and wrote; the two-hour flight flew by!

After she received my list, she called and asked me to talk to her about the things on the list. I felt important and noticed. She had devised a simple but very effective technique for determining what to reinforce.

Since that time years ago, I've enjoyed making the same kind of list for myself. Every now and then, I sit and jot down the things I'm proud of — and feel good.

We start knowing our work is important —
when other people tell us.

Fighting Your Way To The Top

I DARE SAY that most people who have had many promotions within their organization are somewhat self-motivated. They are what we sometimes call "self-starters." They don't require a lot of outside recognition to be able to do what they do on their jobs every day. If they needed a lot of external reinforcers to advance and progress and continually improve, they probably wouldn't be in responsible positions today. Most of them will acknowledge that with the old negative system, they didn't receive much external reinforcement as they fought their way up the ladder.

Realistically, many people achieve their status and their goals in spite of much punishment. That they are at their present level with the organization and have the kind of responsibility they have means they are probably able to reinforce themselves. They don't require people coming in and saying, "Hey, I like what you did over there." They probably wouldn't have progressed if they had depended solely on someone else's opinion. They were able to scavenge to find their own reinforcement and . . . they brought along a supply of their own.

So what's the problem with this? People who get to the higher levels of an organization may be there because they don't need much recognition from others. Consequently, they may tend not to give it.

This doesn't mean that self-reinforcers don't need recognition. They love it just like anyone else. Yet, if they don't get a lot of reinforcement from outside sources, they can manufacture it from within or can find it in their environment. In the botanical world, self-reinforcers would be cacti. No wonder they sometimes develop prickly exteriors.

Many children grew up with adult role models who never took time to savor success. Instead, these role models always set the goal a notch higher. This teaches the lesson that performance is never good enough. People with this background have a very hard time, during their drive home from work, enjoying the success they've had that day. They're too concerned about what they haven't done, or what they've got to do better tomorrow.

Being goal-oriented or striving for continuous improvement is desirable. But we should pause a few seconds and think about what we do each day that is good. This enables us to say to ourselves, "The way I handled that problem today was all right." We then give ourselves permission to accept recognition without thinking, "I didn't do enough," or "I should have done better." More about this later.

Quality recognition helps us notice the right things that we do, so that we automatically go through that process of self-reinforcement when we repeat those behaviors.

You know you've given quality recognition when you help someone get into the habit of telling herself, "Hey, that's good. I'm proud of that."

Q uality recognition gives people permission to be proud of what they do.

Right Time, Right Place

A CORRELATION EXISTS between how quickly after the performance you reinforce and how influential your reinforcer is. Data shows that the most effective reinforcers are those delivered while the behavior is occurring. The second most effective reinforcers are delivered immediately after the desired behavior occurs.

I am often asked, "How realistic is it to reinforce during the behavior?"

It's very realistic and possible. One way to do this is to spend time among the people you want to reinforce with no purpose other than to look for those positive behaviors. When you walk through an area and notice someone doing something right, such as showing initiative or helping others, that's the time to stop and catch them in the act.

Go up and speak to them, put a hand on their shoulder, or give them a wink or the thumbs-up sign as you pass by. You can do any of these gestures during the behavior. Reinforcing doesn't always mean stopping and saying, "I just noticed what you're doing and I like that." Any signal that you see what someone is doing and that you approve, is reinforcing. By placing yourself physically where the performers are, you'll be able to find many things to reinforce.

For example, you may be waiting to talk to someone when she gets off the phone. Meanwhile, if you pick up from her conversation that she is handling a problem correctly with a customer, you can say, "You handled that well. Good answer," or "Sounds like you were being very patient." This is a good way to reinforce immediately after a desirable behavior occurs.

John Failla, Publisher of *Discount Store News*, was listening to one of his team members, Tony Lisanti, talk about a new performance improvement plan he had initiated. Happy that Tony had selected a very valuable part of the business to try to improve, John said, "That's digging where there's 'taters!'"* Tony smiled and understood that John was placing value on his efforts.

Management by walking around is a popular practice nowadays and many managers try to do it.

Unfortunately, many people interpret it as simply spending time in the work area. Because they were trained to solve problems and troubleshoot, many

---

John credits his colleague, Harry Estes, with this phrase.

managers spend this time looking for problems and talking to people about those problems. What you do while you're wandering around determines the difference between negative and positive management. Are you recognizing what people are doing right or are you using that time to correct and issue instructions?

Dr. John B. Davis, in his cassette tape, "Ten Actions of the Best People Managers," recommends taking a minimum of ten minutes during the day to do nothing but look for positive things. As he puts it, "Go on a reinforcement tour." We can all do this whether or not we manage someone else.

Wander without an agenda in mind . . . simply show up in the work area and purposefully look for what people are doing well. A strong reinforcer for many of us is as simple as having someone show up where we are and know what we're doing.

*W*ander with reinforcement and recognition in mind.

Giving Of Yourself

ONE OF MY FIRST JOBS was with a 24-hour-a-day manufacturing operation. It was our policy around Thanksgiving and Christmas to serve a catered meal to every shift. The supervisors and managers showed up to serve the food themselves. This was the element that made the meals special.

Employees enjoyed the food, but they appreciated the occasions for a reason other than the enjoyment of eating. They knew the managers had come in from spending time with their families. They knew that some of the managers had set their alarms at 2:00 a.m. to come to the plant and serve a meal at 3:30 a.m. That was meaningful to people. Giving your time impresses anybody, because everyone realizes how valuable time, especially personal time, is.

Also, everyone enjoys some one-on-one attention. Giving your time and attention sends the message, "I made an effort to spend time with you. This is not a meeting. I'm not doing this out of obligation. I put aside five minutes in my schedule today to come and sit and talk with you about some things you did well." Or, "I'm here to listen, if you want to talk to me about some of the things you're doing."

Give your time selectively. The time the managers gave to serve meals at the holidays made the statement, "I care enough to be with you while you're working on Christmas Day." This did not specifically reinforce good performance; it reinforced whatever was happening at the time.

Give your attention to those behaviors in others which you value. This is a much wiser use of your time, since you'll be increasing whatever behaviors you attend to.

Time is the most valuable thing we can give to one another. Your time is what you give when you pause over someone's work with a smile on your face.

There is no present like the time.

Face-To-Face

SOME PEOPLE ENJOY PUBLIC RECOGNITION, and some don't. The best rule is: While people are still forming opinions about being recognized, don't single one out as a good example in front of the group. You might embarrass him and you may unintentionally set him up in a competitive relationship with peers.

Some people feel that public recognition makes them appear as apple polishers. With private reinforcement you eliminate the risk of inadvertently punishing such an individual in front of his peer group. Please don't conclude that you should never publicly acknowledge someone's accomplishments. However, using private recognition is one way to make sure you miss this pitfall until you know more about an individual's preference.

One organization's managers learned this lesson the hard way when arranging a banquet to honor employee attendance. The division vice president would present awards with a great deal of hoopla. Chauffeured limousines were reserved to pick up award recipients at their homes. A technician who had not missed a day of work in 13 years was to receive special recognition. On banquet day that technician — the star guest — called in sick.

What a coincidence.

Managers later discovered that he was embarrassed by all this, and would rather do almost anything than go to the fancy dinner in a chauffeured limousine.

How can we, then, give recognition to our valued employees? Jack Weller, Performance Manager at PPG Fiber Glass in Lexington, North Carolina, tells about one way:

> In participative management programs, or self-directed work teams, we use the power of the individual's knowledge and experience by letting employees handle everyday problems. Your trust in them to handle these situations is a natural reinforcer to them. They decide which problems to kick upstairs.

Many people with years of experience on the same job take pride in their craftsmanship and professionalism. They are proud of what they do. If they have a negative reaction to the reinforcement we try to give, it's because we are giving them what we think they should want.

Think about those last two words . . . "should want," an oxymoron* if there's ever been one.

Often the real reinforcer they want is to be individually, and usually privately, recognized for their skill, their experience, and their knowledge. So many people from all levels and professions include on their personal reinforcer lists: "Ask me my opinion. Talk to me about my project. Let me in on things."

The best reinforcer you can give this type of person is to ask him sincerely, in private, his opinion about how to handle a problem related to his field. Let him know you value what he has to offer.

*A*ck me my opinion.

An oxymoron is a phrase which sounds like a contradiction in terms, such as jumbo shrimp, almost perfect, or pretty ugly.

Stand Alone Recognition

*A*FTER WE REINFORCE SOMEONE we may yield to the temptation to say, "Now, tell me what happened when you talked to so-and-so about that deadline." Asking about the status of another project detracts from a well-intentioned reinforcer, even when you're not asking for additional behavior.

Even if your questions or remarks are non-punishing information, you are changing the focus. In doing so, you force the recipient to abandon the conversation that was making her feel good. It's as though you're saying, "You've had enough time to feel good. Now let's get on to real business."

If you make a phone call or have a meeting for no other purpose than to reinforce, you convey the message, "I have time to give you for something you did that I like." Then your reinforcer is apparently not an afterthought or something that you thought of on your way over as a smooth conversation opener. This stand-alone delivery adds strength to the reinforcement, because it's the only communication the person hears from you at that time.

When you walk away, leave her with only your positive comments to remember. It's better for her to have time to soak it in, to wallow in that reinforcement, than to be thinking about whatever else the conversation led to.

Sometimes when you talk to someone about what you liked, she may voluntarily give you more information about the project. If that happens, go with it. What the individual may be telling you is, "I can get even more reinforcement from this conversation if you will listen and let me give you more detail about how I achieved this." When she takes the conversation in another direction after you've reinforced her, she may be saying, "While you're here, let me tell you about another thing I'm proud of."

People do tell you about what they've been working on in order to update you. Sure, they want to inform you, but secretly . . . they want to tell you about something else that might earn them more recognition.

If this happens, you don't have to respond by doing anything complicated or difficult. Just stand there and listen — with interest, and respond naturally.

Take care not to listen to non-productive complaining or negative talk about other people in the organization. You could be accidentally indicating your approval for the wrong behavior if the conversation gets off-track.

The key to successful stand-alone reinforcement is to keep it positive and to let it soak in without interference. Give the receiver time to savor and enjoy it. Don't muddy the water by tossing in another issue. Stand-alone delivery introduces and subtly eases people onto the path of self-reinforcement, as they relive the experience that made them feel good.

Whatever you listen to, you'll get more of.

Lead-Ins To Universal Praise

*U*SING A POSITIVE STATEMENT ABOUT A SPECIFIC PERFORMANCE as a lead-in to more universal praise is a sure-fire way to make someone's day. It's also a way to lead them into more self-reinforcement.

The lead-in method starts with comments about a specific behavior a person does that you like. This comment leads to a generalization that will serve as a universal and important reinforcer to that person.

For example, if you like the way an individual meets a deadline, you might say, "I know this was a lot of work, but you got it to me on the day that you promised. I appreciate that." You can make this statement even more memorable by adding, "But I shouldn't be surprised, because if you say you'll get something done on a certain date, you always do. I always know that I can depend on you." Of course you only say all of this if it is indeed true.

Now you have used a specific reinforcer as a lead-in to tell that person why he is valuable to you. Of course, reinforcers must be specific. This means don't limit your remark to, "Hey, you're doing a great job. We couldn't do without you." Cite a specific example first. Then you won't leave the receiver wondering why you said what you did.

Other universal follow-up statements might be: "You always do these things so well." "You're very professional." "You present a good image for our department." Once again, use such comments only after making a positive comment about the specific behavior.

Art, a manager, uses this technique very well. One morning he made this statement to Patsy, his secretary of many years: "Patsy, I like what you're wearing today. In fact, you always dress stylishly. Your appearance always conveys the image of the very professional secretary that you are."

Whoa! Do you think Patsy let that remark run through her head a few hundred more times that day? If Art had simply said, "I like your dress," she may not have been pleased. She might even have been slightly annoyed. Patsy is a professional after all, and she also wants recognition for her work. But how could anyone take offense or, for that matter, not take pride in Art's sincere words?

First, he mentioned a specific behavior that he noticed and could reinforce: Patsy dresses stylishly. So he said, "Patsy, I like what you're wearing today." He reinforced at an immediate, right now, and appropriate time. Then Art added a very important piece of information. After naming the specific behavior, he commented on a generalized characteristic. Patsy dresses like the professional secretary she is.

General remarks alone rarely have the positive effect you want. You might say, "Steve, you do such a good job all the time I don't know what we'd do without you. You just do great."

What's wrong with that? First, Steve doesn't know what behavior to do tomorrow to evoke that response from you again. Secondly, if he can't connect your remark to anything in particular, he may decide you're just blowing smoke or possibly being sarcastic. You may even reinforce the wrong behavior. Steve may have just returned from a three martini lunch!

Think of it this way. If you can name a specific behavior that someone does or has done, and go on to say, "This conveys your professionalism, your diligence, your eye for detail," then you've done a good job of reinforcing. You are telling that person, "This specific event is indicative of something I'm proud of about your habits and I like the way you run your life." Who couldn't use hearing a remark like that once in a while?

You don't have to add the second step. Without it, a specific, positive comment alone still works. If you're into fine-tuning your recognition and reinforcement, however, including that second step is the way to clinch the deal.

Sandy Stewart has been with our organization for years. One thing we all know about Sandy is that she is an excellent negotiator. If something can be obtained at a lower cost, or more can be gotten for our money, Sandy can get it. She derives reinforcement from this. I can tell by the look on her face and her behavior when, after she gets a good deal, I notice it and mention it to her. All I have to say is, "Sandy, you got a price on that I can't believe. I should have known, though. You always do."

By tying a general comment to a specific behavior, you prove to the performer that she has earned the reputation as a professional secretary, a great visionary, a good chauffeur, an excellent implementer, and so on. Someone's else's words are now in that person's memory and that memory says, "You came through for us, and not just this time. You always do."

One of the things I have on my reinforcer survey* is to be given the opportunity to work on important projects. Therefore, in my case, asking me to do more work happens to reinforce me. At one time my boss asked me to do something that had not been done before, (a sort of put-this-together-and-try-and-make-it-work project). He said, "I want you to be the one to do this, because you're the person who can make it happen. You always do."

---

*A list of things which would provide meaningful recognition for me personally. This list is shared with all my co-workers and boss.

Getting the assignment was one reinforcer, but the other words added sparkle to the reinforcer. My boss let me know he had confidence in me, that he trusted me with the project. Then he told me the reason for that trust, rather than saying, "because you're the only person around right now." I ran his words through my head for the rest of the week.

We often have opportunities to reinforce people. Two prime examples of common opportunities are when we select someone for a special project or when we promote someone. We select certain individuals for certain activities for definite reasons. We miss opportunities to reinforce them because we don't take the time to say, "And the reason I think you're the best person for the job is . . . ."

You've gone through that thought process before you asked the person to do it, so go ahead and take one more minute to share your reasons with them.

*C*onnect the specific behavior to the general pattern.

Peer Positives

*R*EINFORCEMENT OFTEN COMES FROM PEERS and can be as important as recognition from your manager. Several of my
experiences illustrate this fact.

After I completed a presentation to a group of clients,
which included quite a bit of group participation, Ann
Pinney, one of my colleagues, said, "I noticed so many
things you did to help people feel safe about participating. These people have to go back to their organizations
and do that same kind of facilitating. I wonder if they're
picking up on all the things you do that work. What if we
had a session to ask them to identify the things you did
to encourage their participation?"

Ann then led a group exercise asking seminar attendees to list the things I did to encourage and reinforce

their participation. They listed simple and subtle things such as picking up a marker when someone began to talk, writing down a point made by a participant, and walking toward a person to indicate my interest and to draw the group's attention his way.

She and my audience then listed specific behaviors in my teaching methods, an exercise which was very reinforcing to me. The reinforcement value for me was the realization that, "Somebody noticed the little things I do."

Often, we're only told what not to do, leaving us without a clue about what is expected of us or what we do correctly. Ann's main intention was to lead a 15-minute exercise which taught people how to pinpoint behaviors for encouraging group participation. While her session was successful in doing this, it was also successful in making me feel great.

Now you wouldn't do this particular exercise in most meetings, but you can do less elaborate, but effective things. If you are aware that someone has been working hard to polish their presentation skills, you can reinforce their efforts. After all, those meeting-type behaviors are fragile. Follow that person straight back to her office after the meeting and say, "I want to tell you all the things you did to make that presentation go well." Or give her a smile, a wink, or a thumbs-up during her presentation.

In some of our seminars, we, as team teachers, take notes on our colleagues' presentations, listing everything we like about their teaching techniques. Later we talk to them about our lists and give them our written comments so they'll have them for reference. Everyone enjoys this. Comments like these can come from your colleagues or even someone who doesn't know your job that well. When they pinpoint your nuances, and specific methods, it's similar to an "aha" experience. Only this time the light bulb in your head says, "They noticed!"

Byron Chandler, Consultant, related a story about a course he took which required quite a bit of detailed pre-work. In the course description, the instructor stated that he would recognize any student's efforts to prepare for the course.

On the first morning of class, Byron was surprised when the instructor began giving M&M candies to each person who demonstrated knowledge of the material. By morning's end, each student had accumulated a sizable pile of candy.

It was approximately two hours into the course before the students began rewarding one another with M&Ms. This demonstrates that when people accumulate enough reinforcement, they then feel comfortable giving it to others.

It also shows that we shouldn't assume reinforcement must come predominantly from the "person in charge" — the one who writes the review, does the appraisals, or teaches the class. When people start getting reinforcement from their peers they realize its importance to them. They discover a whole new dimension of recognition and reinforcement.

Peer reinforcement is generally very appealing to most people, possibly because there is rarely any question whether reinforcement from peers is sincere. If you get recognition from your peers you're likely to think it came from the heart, because you know they don't have to do it. Also, they know what you do every day. They are right there beside you in the trenches. That co-worker knows the behaviors you went through to make a project successful, whereas sometimes the manager only sees the results of your labors.

Peer recognition is not more important than recognition from the manager. Yet, there are so many more opportunities for us to receive reinforcement if we also receive it from our peers — opportunities that would be a shame to waste.

H ave you reinforced a buddy today?

The Hatfields And
The McCoys

O FTEN A GROUP WORKS TOGETHER REGULARLY in a self-managed team. Management wants them to reach the point where it is not always the responsibility of a supervisor or a manager to reinforce them. Indeed, a self-managed team is hard-pressed to stay together as a functioning unit, unless at least some peer reinforcement exists.

Again, self-reinforcement is a good goal, but the conver sion process to total self-reinforcement may take one to several years. Any team consists of individuals, and most of us have such a deficit in reinforcement that we require reinforcement repair. We have to get filled up from an outside source. Only then can we start doing more of it for ourselves.

Before you can even begin encouraging peers to re-inforce one another, you must make sure they are not already in an adversarial relationship. One manager told me about a pair of operators who had been at one another's throats for years. He doesn't even know when or why the battle started, but the constant backbiting was annoying to the manager and to co-workers. Still, apart from their constant one-upmanship and mutual undermining of one another's work, they were excellent employees.

He wanted to know, "How do you break up a Hatfields-and-McCoys trend?" Even if you could stifle the sniping, how do you get them to reinforce one another?

Well, it's going to take some time.

You will have to act as a go-between. One thing to do, whenever you can, is pick up on something that Hatfield says that, in any way, is a small, positive statement about McCoy. You may have to elicit these remarks with prompts like, "I understand you and McCoy worked together on this project. How did it go?" Even if he only answers, "Well I did this and McCoy did that," you've got your plug. You can now go to McCoy and say, "Hatfield told me you both worked on this project and he said you did this." You can then put your own positive spin on the fact which Hatfield reported to you. Now McCoy knows that Hatfield at least gave you the facts to enable you to reinforce.

One manager faced this same problem with two high-level engineers. Each of the engineers spent time in his office (separately) at least once a week, telling him about the faults and inadequacies of the other. Finally he gave the engineers an assignment. He asked each of them to write one positive, specific statement every week about the performance of the other. Then he shared the good news with each of them. Gradually, he built their relationship until he was able to drop out as mediator. Today, over a year later, they support each other and work well together.

If there is any hint of a reinforcer that you can pass on to McCoy from Hatfield (and vice versa), use it. Then you will start to break down those barriers. This is positive gossip or third-person reinforcement. Convey to person A that B recognizes what he does (even if B isn't overflowing with love and admiration). Then gradually shape them into reinforcing one another by applauding any semblance of teamwork between them.

*M*ost of us require reinforcement repair.

Birds Of A Feather Or
Manager To Manager

*M*ANAGERS ARE OFTEN THE WORST OFFENDERS when it comes to neglecting the important area of peer reinforcement. Many managers think, "Well, I didn't have to have all this recognition stuff when I was coming up." They translate this to mean they don't need to give recognition to people who are at their same level or to the people who report directly to them. These managers can go onto the floor and reinforce front-line employees, but people on their own level? "Nah, they don't need it because they're a lot like me."

This assumption is probably, for the most part, true. The managers and direct reports will of course survive without your reinforcement, but they will never realize the full potential of positive reinforcement until they share reinforcement with their employees and peers.

One of my clients, a company president, made a valuable observation about reinforcing. He realized one day that his entire focus, and that of his direct reports, was on reinforcing the front-line crews. The supervisors and middle managers had been entirely left out of the reinforcement loop. There were no plans for reinforcing managers, only plans for them to reinforce their direct reports.

Luckily, he quickly realized something that too few people realize. "We have to reinforce the people who work directly for and with us," he said. "They're the ones we depend on to reinforce everyone else."

*R*ecognition begins at home.

Positive Gossip

OUR CONSULTING DIVISION VICE PRESIDENT CALLED ME ONE DAY and said, "We have a new client. Your boss and I were talking about it and we think you'd be good at working with them." He went on to tell me why. Sounds simple, but many people don't realize the reinforcing value of repeated positive remarks. We usually think of gossip as saying nasty, dirty, negative things behind someone's back. Yet, when someone says something good about another person and I tell that person about it, she seems to get more reinforcement value from it than if she had received the compliment firsthand.

Think about it. First, you know if someone says something positive about you to someone else, that person must be sincere. If the person who heard the comment then repeats it to you, you know it passed through her head. Now a reinforcing comment about you and the quality of your work is in her memory, also. As a result, you get reinforcement from two people instead of one.

Katie Muldoon, a client, has relayed positive gossip to me on several occasions. Once, when I was traveling with my boss, Aubrey Daniels, and Wilson Rourk, a fellow consultant, I went to my hotel room before dinner, made a call, and picked up the messages on my home answering machine. Katie's voice was the first I heard. Her message was, "Janis, I didn't know where I could reach you and I didn't want to wait any longer to tell you this."

Katie had been talking with some attendees from a session Aubrey and I had taught together the previous week. Three vice presidents from her company had attended, and Katie scouted around for their impressions about the session later. She told me there were many positive comments and repeated some of them. Then she said, "One of the vice presidents told me he had never met you before, but after your presentation remarked, 'It's good to know there is that kind of depth backing Aubrey in the organization.'"

My biggest problem at the moment was that I couldn't remember how to rewind my answering machine from long distance and listen to that message over and over again.

That evening, Aubrey, Wilson and I went out for pizza. There are so many decisions to be made when you order pizza: toppings, crust thickness, large or small, anchovies. . . . I thought the waitress would never finish taking our orders and get out of the way. I was dying to tell my news. When she did leave the table, I told them everything. Aubrey jumped in and said, "That's great. You did do a good job and I felt good about leaving the session in your hands when I left mid-week." Additionally, since I was able to repeat the compliment in Wilson's presence (without being too embarrassed), I derived even more reinforcement from it.

After dinner, Wilson said, "That was good news from New York and I'm proud of you."

His remark was reinforcing because it made me aware that he heard what I said and it was on his mind later.

You do want to reinforce as immediately as you can. Yet if you go back after a period of time and say something, other than your initial remarks, it tells that person, "You made an impression on me."

By spreading positive gossip Katie not only reinforced me, but gave me the chance to get more reinforcement when I shared the positive comments with others. For me, the entire experience was one of quality recognition.

An Example Of Positive Gossip
From Electronic Mail . . .

Tue 6-Mar-90 10:41am
JDaniels informed
To   GSnyder
Subject   Articles
Categories magazine
Cc   Director

Tom Wilson, our new guy in Boston, just sold a pilot program to a hospital in Boston. He says that what clinched it was your article "How To Reinforce a Neurosurgeon."

Congratulations. This is the kind of impact we hope to get from the magazine. I know that it happens often but I thought you might like to hear about this one.

You wrote a good one.

Referent Reinforcement

In a piece of written feedback on his techniques as an instructor, I wrote to one of my clients, John O'Brien, that I found him to be "otherish" (focused on the audience rather than himself). "Otherish," as I explained, is a term coined by Dr. John B. Davis, a fellow consultant. My client replied, "Well, that's particularly reinforcing to me because I respect John Davis very much."

After thinking about his reaction, I realized that this is a first cousin to positive gossip — associating one person's habits with those of someone he admires.

Surprise . . . You're It!

*P*LANNED REINFORCEMENT IS FINE, but unplanned reinforce ment can be fun. The planned-reinforcement trap is easy to fall into, especially when you structure your reinforcement plan around results only.

Keep in mind, if you set up reinforcement around weekly results, no law says you must wait until Friday to celebrate. If you discover on Wednesday that your team is at or above the level you expect it to be at week's end, don't hesitate. Have an on-the-spot celebration. Then if you want, celebrate again on Friday. This lets people know you're watching; you're paying attention; you're on top of it. It gives them the message, "Don't miss a day of work because you never know what good things you may miss around here." Unpredictability adds an air of anticipation to every day.

People often say they prefer surprise (or unexpected) reinforcement to planned reinforcement. With planned reinforcement, you set a goal and you celebrate in some way when and if you meet the goal. Everybody knows ahead of time what to expect and when.

People like for somebody to pay attention to what they do toward meeting that goal. People need to know that reinforcement is not just something you give mechanically because the graph numbers tell you it's time. When someone shows up in the middle of the day and says, "I just heard about something good you did," it simply makes coming to work more enjoyable.

Many organizations have annual performance appraisals. Employees know that once a year their supervisor or manager will sit down with them and give an overview on their performance. We have monthly matrix reviews at my company, so an end-of-the-year appraisal would be a surprise. This set the scene for a memorable reinforcer which happened to me.

It was on New Year's Eve day. I had been on a new job assignment for nine months. At the end of the day my boss came in, sat down, and said, "I just want you to know what I think of your work since you've been on this new job." Then he went on to say some positive and specific things.

He took the time to review my activities over the past nine months. The very idea of it made me feel good.

Though many people see job reviews or appraisals as negative experiences, this surprise review was positive for me. Because it came as such a surprise, and a pleasant one, I'll always remember it.

You never know what fun things might happen around here.

II.

Why Isn't This Stuff
Working?

*T*HERE ARE MANY OBSTACLES IN THE PATH OF REINFORCEMENT. The major obstacle is that attempts at recognition may not be received well, even though the person making the effort may have the best of intentions.

A phrase used sometimes in counseling to describe interpersonal miscommunications is, "I sent a circle, but you received a square." I like this phrase, because it graphically reminds me that often people are sincerely making the effort to give what they think is a reinforcer, but the receiver doesn't see it that way. At the beginning stages many honest efforts to reinforce fail because we send a circle and someone receives a square.

Part Of The Masses

ONE COMPANY'S MANAGERS CALCULATED that, in one particular quarter, the company achieved the highest sales in its history. So, they decided to have a big celebration for their several thousand employees. They printed up cases and cases of coffee mugs and packed them along with a cover letter, which they sent to each department. All managers and department heads were instructed to distribute the mugs at a specific time and to read the memo explaining the reason.

It was such a massive reinforcement attempt that it appeared impersonal. Furthermore, hardly any of the people who received these things had any idea why. They had not been reinforced along the way for any of their contributions for meeting this goal. All they understood was, "We, as a company, sold more of our product. Good, maybe we have more job security."

They hadn't known that a goal existed, what they had done to attain that goal, or what they could do to help maintain and surpass future company goals. To most employees, meeting the goal had more to do with market conditions, or the sales force, than it did with their own behaviors. The mug was also the first recognition they could remember ever having received.

Since this tangible item was the only reinforcer they had ever received, they mistakenly wondered, "Is this how they value my contribution? This coffee mug costs two or three bucks! We have record breaking sales and this is all they're giving me?"

This reinforcer took them by surprise. This doesn't suggest that surprise tangible reinforcement doesn't work, but this particular reinforcer fell out of the sky with no message about what they did to earn it. Sure the company achieved top sales, but what did that have to do with each of the individuals who received a coffee mug?

It's tempting for people to give this type of reinforcer, because when an organization breaks a record it seems that everybody should be excited about it. The numbers tell you it's time to reinforce and you want to share it with everyone in the company. The natural inclination is to say, "Wow, this is record-breaking time, the four-minute mile. Let's celebrate!"

Though the intentions are the best, this doesn't come across as personal to people whose jobs aren't directly connected to the number you're celebrating.

When considering group reinforcers, one might keep in mind Queen Victoria's comment about Gladstone. She said, "He speaks to me as if I were a public meeting."

*C*ast out the "cast of thousands" reinforcers.

Saying "Reinforcement" Doesn't Make It Happen

A SHORTHAND WAY TO EXPRESS POSITIVE REINFORCEMENT is with the symbol "R+." One client related one of the worst (and possibly funniest) misuses of this term. His story is as follows:

> The term "R+" is probably the most abused word in our plant. People will put up a graph and say, "Boy, look here. We've gone six weeks without a defect. R-plus!"
>
> Instead of congratulating the performers they simply say, "R+." Or they say, "Hey guys, I want to R+ you on that."
>
> That's it! It's like, "Okay, give it to me, then." Yet nothing ever happens. Believe me, I could show you hundreds of examples of this in one day.

One fellow even shouted, "R+ all round." Whenever this happens, it's like throwing candy off a train.

As funny as this may sound, it probably isn't that humorous to the performers. Shouting "R+" does nothing to focus on the individual, the behavior, or the result. These managers have confused the word with the action. Believe it or not, this happens frequently. Remember, the term R+ is not something you say, it's something you do.

*T*alking about it isn't doing it.

The Downfield Pass

A WELL-KNOWN AND PROMINENT POLITICIAN is rumored never to have uttered a self-written word in his life. Even at the funeral of his own brother, he asked a speech writer to compose the eulogy for him saying, "Write something sad."

Well, maybe the writer did a good job and maybe no one at the funeral knew that the words were not the politician's own. If his brother could hear, he would know.

Please don't ask someone else to do your reinforcing for you. This gets back to the old, "The company appreciates your performance," line. "The company expects you to do this." Policy manuals are usually written this way: "It is the expectation of the company that you...."

To individuals, there is no such thing as a company or a corporation as an entity. An organization is a group of people, of individuals.

My daddy was a supervisor in a textile plant for 42 years. I remember listening to his telephone conversations with his employees. He supervised the second shift, which started at 2:30 p.m. When I was home from school in the summer, his employees sometimes interrupted our lunch to call in sick or talk about this problem or that. So I got my first impression of what management was by hearing only one side of the telephone calls — the supervisor's side.

I noticed that Daddy always used the word "we" when he meant "I."

"Well, we need you."

"Well, we'll let you go home later if you come in and you don't start feeling better."

He had received training that taught him, "Don't use 'I.' Use 'we.'" The whole mentality around this is, "It's the company. I'm not taking responsibility for the negatives or the positives." That approach spills over into the reinforcing process. People say, "We appreciate what you do around here."

One business video aptly demonstrates this. In the video, a manager walks around shaking every employee's hand as he drones, "Good job fella, Acme appreciates it." He repeats the same line to everyone. Even the women get, "Good job fella, Acme appreciates it." He ends his goodwill tour by shaking the hand of a cardboard cut-out Santa saying, "Good job fella, Acme appreciates it."

This farce comes all too close to reality in many companies. One supervisor told me that once when his division achieved a goal, the division vice president decided it was time for a celebration. So he wrote a letter and had hundreds printed, one for each employee. He didn't want to mail these letters, though. He wanted them handed to each individual, but he didn't have the time to do that.

So every supervisor who came in that morning had 20 or more copies of the letter from Mr. Big in the mailbox with a cover note that read, "Please hand these to all employees and congratulate them for their work."

Well, the supervisors hated it. It wasn't their idea and the letter wasn't from them. Yet, each one of them was stuck with saying, "Mr. Big wrote this letter and wants me to give it to you along with his congratulations."

Mr. Big meant well. He was probably thinking, "If the supervisor gives the letter out, he or she will be in on the reinforcer and will personalize it." He didn't think that supervisors would toss the letters on a table or put them in the break area for people to pick up. But that's just what some of them did. The whole plan backfired. The pervasive, though unspoken message, from most of the supervisors was, "My mother made me do it."

*T*his recognition comes from me to you.

The Data Made Me Do It

*T*HE EASIEST WAY TO SET UP REINFORCEMENT is at the end of some scheduled point of measurement. Usually when a person writes a performance improvement plan he says, "Well, at the end of the week I'll go around and tell everybody I appreciate what they've been doing." Then he does it again at the end of two weeks, the end of the month, or whatever. Eventually, he gets on a regular maintenance schedule for giving recognition. Once a week or once a month he looks at the data and reinforces.

After a period of time his schedule is very predictable. When the reinforcement comes, people know they have earned it, and it makes them feel good about the improvements they've made. But if this is the only type of reinforcement people get, it quickly becomes de-personalized for the individual. It's almost like, "Well, it's Christmas, so of course you had to buy me a turkey."

Finally the performers get the impression that when the report comes out you have to have a celebration or you have to come around and talk to everyone. The sentiment may become, "Reinforcing us is not something you want to do."

We will never mold self-reinforcing individuals as long as we reinforce only results. By reinforcing behaviors, we give a person the opportunity to see what someone else likes about her work. In turn, she is now more likely to engage in a little silent, enjoyable session of patting herself on the back whenever she repeats those behaviors.

The way to add personal value to recognition is to make sure that people receive attention for good performance daily, not only at the close of a measurement interval. If you only reinforce results, then people are going to feel that only the graph on the wall prompts reinforcement.

Value me, not just my results.

"Here's A Nickel — Don't Blow It All In One Place"

I THINK PEOPLE EMPHASIZE TANGIBLE REINFORCEMENT (material items) because often the company provides tangible items for them to give out. If someone in the company has printed up T-shirts as a reinforcer, those items are accessible, no-hassle ways to reinforce. The giver can always say, "Well, sure I reinforced her. I gave her a T-shirt."

If people receive mostly tangible reinforcers, they will focus on the dollar value of those reinforcers. They may become unhappy with them, because they will compare the dollar value of the item with the value of their contributions. Then, they become picky and start probing to see what people in other departments receive. "They got jackets and we only got T-shirts," is a popular whine.

To avoid this detrimental atmosphere, de-emphasize the tangibles. The best approach is not to use them at all until people get the idea that reinforcement is predominantly a social type of recognition.

Surprisingly, many people say they wish their organizations would give fewer tangibles and more social reinforcers.

Every group differs, but often, after I've explained the difference between social, tangible, and work-activity reinforcers, many people say they prefer to throw tangibles out the window. They see so many problems with using them. Most people are hungry for somebody to simply look them in the eye and say, "I like the way you do that."

A friend of mine, Ruth Ackermann, learned about reinforcement when she taught a Sunday School class a few years ago. At first she was simply trying to get the children to attend, then to bring their Bibles. Later, she reinforced their behavior to the point that they were reading their lessons and memorizing scriptures.

Experiencing this success, she decided to try recognition methods with her own six- and seven-year-olds to encourage them to read more during the summer. It was during this effort she learned a valuable lesson about tangible versus social reinforcers.

Ruth wanted her children to read good books so she made up a long reading list and then put together a reinforcement plan for them. For every three books they read, they could reach into a shopping bag of goodies and pull something out. When Ruth began choosing what to put in the reinforcer bag she chose tangible items. What fun things could she wrap up and put in a grab bag?

In her first bag she included little trinkets, toys, and candy. Later, she added little prizes for herself and for the family. The idea was to create, not simply the joy of receiving, but the spirit of celebrating an accomplished goal. She was surprised to find that the children got as much enjoyment pulling out an item for the family as they did grabbing a prize for themselves. The real reinforcer was the celebration, the right to pull the item from the bag, not the item itself.

The symbolic value of a tangible is all important. Most of us have seen a framed dollar bill hanging on the wall of a restaurant. Usually that dollar is the first dollar made by the establishment. The owner protects it behind glass and hangs it proudly for all his customers to see. The work that went into earning that first dollar, the reward or receiving that first bill from the first paying customer, means much more to the owner than the exchange rate of the currency.

One morning in a restaraunt as I shared breakfast with two clients from an organization in Brazil, I witnessed a similar circumstance. I told my Brazilian friends, Elmano and Ze Carlos that before returning to their country they should really try the southern dish, grits. Elmano promptly ordered "a grit." Our waitress, Beverly Lee, thought this was funny, and teased him about it. A conversation about Brazil followed.

"Wait a minute now," said Beverly. "Isn't Brazil the country that doesn't speak Spanish, like the rest of South America, but Portuguese?" Elmano was surprised. "You know, very few people in the U.S. know that. That's very good!"

Beverly smiled proudly and said, "Yeah, I know. I always win at Jeopardy." Ze Carlos reached into his wallet and took out a cruzado (Brazilian currency). Handing her the bill, he said, "I want you to keep this, because you are so smart and know so much about Brazil."

She looked at it and beamed. Suddenly a busboy clearing the next table, spotted the bill and walked over. Coming up behind Beverly, he literally rested his chin on her shoulder to get a better view of the bill. "What's that?" he asked. She told him, and the two walked toward the kitchen, talking all the way.

About that time Ze Carlos glanced toward the kitchen door and remarked, "Look at the commotion." A crowd of Beverly's co-workers had gathered to look at the Brazilian bill and hear Beverly's story.

Later, I said to Beverly, "You know you can take that money to a bank and they will exchange it for you in U.S. dollars."

Her reply, "Oh no, I'm going to keep this one " The money wasn't to be spent, but to be a symbol.

When I was a performance manager at a manufacturing company, people thought my job description was "holder of the keys to the goody closet." Unfortunately, early on we got excited over the trinkets and whatnots that we could have printed with the company logo. We had pocket knives, key chains, sun visors, beach towels, T-shirts — the works.

We also had approximately 2,000 employees in that plant and quite a few supervisors. When the loom fixers did this, we gave them a key chain. When the maintenance people did that, we handed them a pocket knife. This is how we operated our "positive reinforcement" plan. It got to the point that one supervisor came to me and said, "I need to get Harold to work overtime this weekend. Do you have anything I can give him?"

I knew then it was time to do something differently.

If your reinforcement plan has degenerated into this scenario, it's time to make some changes. As wrong as it sounds, this occurs quite frequently. Why? Because, it's difficult to get those crusty old supervisors and managers to look someone in the eye and say, "I'm proud of you."

That's scary! So, in our case, we handed them a trinket and said, "Here, go give this to somebody."

Then we could all go home.

"It's amazing how many writers stay in the business just for the by-line," remarked Jeff Arlen, Executive Editor of *Apparel Merchandising*. When I asked Jeff if I could use his remark in this book he laughed, "Sure, I'm just in it for the quotes."

The real value of a tangible is its social value, the story behind it, the recognition it represents.

Milt Berwin, a Senior Art Director, recently showed me his personal performance improvement plan, a written blueprint for improving one's own performance. As we discussed it I looked down and absent-mindedly pulled a loose string from the bottom of my skirt. As a joke I looped it into the shape of a "J," taped it to the bottom of his written plan, and called it "Janis' Seal of Approval."

Milt leaned back in his chair and laughed, then said, "I'll bet I've got the only one of those?" Then with his head down and looking up through his eyebrows he added with mock seriousness, "Keep it low, okay?"

I think that was New York talk for, "Don't spread this around," but a few minutes later he gave me permission to put this story in this book.

*A*nything can be a reinforcer, even a string!

Results Are All I Smile For

*R*ESULTS ARE WHAT COMPANIES LIVE AND DIE BY, so I'm all for improving results. That's how we stay in business. It is often true that if the company does well, then so do its employees. If results are the only emphasis, however, recognition quickly moves away from the individual. That's one reason why we must reinforce behaviors and celebrate results.

"Our sales volume is up this month!"

"Congratulations, our quality has improved to a 99.3 percent level."

These statements highlight results. When we recognize only results we focus solely on what's good for the company. We do nothing to let the individual see the value in what he did.

People generate results. Therefore we must reinforce individual as well as group performance.

If we do this, then we're sure to examine what individuals do, not just what is left over at the end of the day after they've completed all the necessary work behaviors. As mentioned previously, to focus on behavior we must go out and find what people are doing right. This means we have to make personal contact with them. When we get this information directly from them, we won't have to limit our reinforcer to a letter that says, "We met our goals this week. Thank you."

Remember, focusing on behavior requires time and energy from you. To do it right you have to be there. You have to see what the person does. You have to stand in the same five-foot diameter circle with him.

*R*einforcing the right behaviors —
leads to the right results.

Show Biz

I NEVER DID TRUST THAT GUY. At times people have told me they suspect their manager's motives for giving group re inforcement — even intangible recognition, such as making an announcement about how well the department is doing. They suspect their manager does this because it's politically the right thing to say in front of an audience — especially if an important executive is present. For some reason, based on their past experience with that supervisor or manager, they doubt her sincerity. "She's only doing that because the company says she has to."

That isn't everyone's perception. Giving recognition to groups in public can work. However, if you make a point to catch someone doing a good job and tell them privately that you like what they are doing, then you will decrease the room for suspicion about your sincerity when you reinforce publicly.

People sometimes don't trust the person trying to reinforce them, for valid reasons. I've heard lines like, "Joe has never said a nice thing in his life. Then he goes to charm school, comes out here, says something he probably memorized, and expects me to think he's a changed man. I know he's just doing this because upper management is on his case to reinforce and he has to report how many reinforcers he gave this week."

A person who has been a constant victim of Joe's negative ways has a right to be a hard sell. That person will be skeptical of Joe's reinforcement efforts for quite a while, especially when reinforcing marks a dramatic change in Joe's usual behavior. If Joe rarely or never reinforced his employees before, why should they believe him now?

If Joe's former relations with his employees have been primarily negative, he may have to prove his sincerity by continuing to reinforce. If he usually spoke to his employees in private only to chew them out, punish or give additional work, he must be patient when his employees eye his reinforcement efforts warily. After all, if after years of negative management, he begins to "make positive" it just won't compute at first. Suddenly Santa's voice is coming out of Oscar the Grouch.

The best advice here is patience and persistence. If Joe's efforts are sincere, and if he continues reinforcing long after "charm school" is over, even the most cynical of his employees will eventually come around to believe he's changed his punishing ways.

Al Hauck, a Performance Manager at Kodak, put it well when he said, "Changing a culture, if it is worth doing, is worth the wait for the persecution to turn to praise! Reinforce the reinforcer."

One way to demonstrate your sincerity is to come right out and admit when you've made a reinforcement gaffe. One executive suddenly realized that upper management wasn't reinforcing supervisors for reinforcing their teams. Yet, he had expected them to keep on keeping on, reinforcing with enthusiasm.

"Well, we had blown it and we were aware of it," he said.

He pulled the troops together and openly and honestly explained his oversight and his plans to correct the problem. Then he spoke with the teams about how they could positively reinforce their supervisors. The open conversation that followed won him a tremendous amount of credibility up and down the employee ladder. It's not always easy to go to somebody and say, "I made a mistake. I'm going to change what I'm doing here." But he saw it as the necessity that it was.

*T*rust takes time and positive experience.

Great Job!
What Do You Do Anyway?

"SHE CAN'T REINFORCE ME, because she doesn't know my job that well."

"They transferred her from a different division into this job and she doesn't know what's going on here."

"He gets these reports and tries to reinforce me, but it doesn't mean anything to me because he doesn't even know what I do."

When people make remarks like these it tells me they want assurance that somebody up there knows they exist. They want some other human being to know what they had to go through to deliver the product on time. It tells me the performer is almost begging for somebody to know enough detail about his job to fully appreciate what it takes to keep it running smoothly.

Does the person giving the reinforcer have to know what you do in order to reinforce you? The performers here aren't saying that the person doing the reinforcing has to be able to do the job or even have hands-on experience doing the job. They're simply asking, "Do you know what I do out here all day . . . or all night?"

This is true for me and my colleagues in the consulting business. We work in relative isolation from one another and from our managers. Reinforcement is valuable to us. We like to know that somebody knows what it takes to have a successful consulting project and knows what we're doing to make that happen.

I suggest that managers try to learn some aspect of every job. They should know some of the necessary behaviors for an operator, but they don't have to know all the parts of a piece of equipment. In addition, managers can learn about what is going on through written reports, from what their direct reports tell them, and even from what they hear through the grapevine.

If it's time to reinforce a person or several people in a department, don't pretend you know the job and don't be afraid to give your attention because you don't know the specific aspects of the job.

Go to the person you want to recognize and be honest. Say, "I see that you have been producing way over goal for three weeks in a row while maintaining quality. Tell me how you're doing it." Then just stand back and listen.

Set that person up to talk about himself and his performance. Most people like to talk about themselves.

They like to talk about their jobs and what they're proud of. This gives them a chance to talk about their successes. That way they can choose what aspects of the job they want to tell you about. And you'll learn something.

If a person chronically complains, constantly telling you how bad life is and how awful things are, it usually signals that he wants to make you aware of his efforts. When he bellyaches, complains, and drives you crazy, he is getting, in a backhanded way, the attention he wasn't getting until he complained. He is finding a way to receive the recognition he wants. When people drag you through every detail of what they do during the day, you may say to yourself, "Why are they doing this? Why do they want to tell me these things?"

Maybe the message you should be receiving is, "You probably think my job is a piece of cake. Let me tell you about all the hurdles I had to jump over to make our department look good."

*M*ost of us eat attention with a spoon.
— *Tony McElwee*

Wonderful Performance!
Now, By The Way . . .

*A*T ONE TIME OR ANOTHER everyone comes into contact with the manager who tells you what a good job you did and how proud he is of your work. Then, in a matter of seconds he adds, "Now the new goal for this month is...."

This very punishing method of "reinforcing" is very difficult for people to resist. In the real world, everyone's time is valuable. It's often difficult to get in touch with people. After you've played telephone tag for two days and you finally see the person, it's almost impossible to avoid giving him every message and directive you've stored up over time. So when you do contact the person and you've got something you want to reinforce him for, why not slip in all the other things you want him to do? What can it hurt?

This is the very tantalizing, "While-I-gotcha" disease. When you do this, and a person already doubts your sincerity, he will probably conclude, "Well, she has a new way of approaching me now. She's going to butter me up, before she tells me she wants me to do more work." Eventually, in this preparing-for-the-kill atmosphere, the performer can't absorb or even recognize the reinforcement. He's too busy worrying about how to handle the rest of the work you're about to drop on him. He begins to believe what Clare Boothe Luce said, "No good deed goes unpunished."

Bud Clay, Vice President of Research and Development at AG Communication Systems, shared the following story about the time when he faced the temptation to reinforce and then ask for more.

> We were trying to have a meeting for all of R&D to talk about the accomplishments of the previous year. We had put a lot into the meeting and we tried to make it interesting, using cartoon characters to highlight the theme of some of the projects. This was intended to be a very uplifting and positive event, because we had done a good job.

> The problem was that we were also looking forward to the coming year. Usually what we had done in the past was say, "Okay you guys have done a great job, but. . .you've got to do an even greater job next year. Things are really going to be tough. We've got to cut this and we've got to improve productivity and quality and so forth."

In the past, management had always sandwiched these things together.

I was concerned that if I didn't ask for higher performance, people would question the value of the meeting. They might say, "There was no toughness; no "Here's how we've got to improve!"

However, we sat down and talked about it and said, "With everything that we've learned in Performance Management, that is not the way to go." We decided to talk about the wonderful accomplishments and to talk about the future, too. But when we talked about the future we talked about the excitement involved in the future and the potential involved for more success. Instead of focusing on advising them to do better, we just said, "We've done great! As a result of that we've got opportunities for all sorts of neat things." We changed our approach from what we had been doing in the past. It was extremely successful.

I was very tempted to revert back to talking about the future in terms of needs, because this was a good opportunity for us, while everybody was in the same room. Later we had individual department meetings to do the future planning, instead. Everybody was very pleased.

In the early days of Performance Management, I used to say, "It's hard for me. It's hard for all of us because we are so used to not taking a minute when we reach a plateau. But we need to take the time to celebrate."

Wonderful performance . . . that's all.

Have An Open-Faced Sandwich

SANDWICHING IS AN INADEQUATE AND DAMAGING WAY OF CORRECTING. Sandwiching happens when the reinforcer first attempts to get on the sandwich victim's good side by finding something about her performance to reinforce. Then he hits her with the bad news about her performance, followed by another positive remark.

Most managers don't enjoy correcting an employee. When faced with the unsavory task, they may try to soft-pedal it. This is an understandable and human, if not cowardly, reaction. Some people add the positive after they have given the negative (or after they've given additional instructions which come across as negative), because they've been trained to do it. They've been told this will protect individual self-esteem. Adding another positive on the end of the sandwich may be an afterthought. Or, the manager may sincerely believe this is the best way to correct.

However, even if sandwiching makes the manager feel more at ease, it does nothing but add strain to the employee/employer relationship.

First, from now on that employee will probably wait for the ax to fall every time the manager makes a positive comment. Also, the reinforcers in a sandwich are immediately shrugged off as insincere and that reputation rubs off on the person doing the sandwiching.

Although many people do use the sandwich approach (a positive, a negative, and a positive) I think that more often people use what Betty Loafmann, my colleague calls, the open-faced sandwich method. That is a positive remark followed by a negative also known as the "yes, but . . . ." This method can be harmful, because the last emphasis is on the negative. Here the performer gets hit with the negative remark and is left holding the bag to boot. For example, one client, a young man in his mid-twenties, said to me, "You've got a lot of energy for a 37-year-old."

Raymond E. Lovett, a writer and psychotherapist, described sandwiching well in his humorous article, "Praise That Hurts." In his article, he wrote about the crippling effect of a dance partner's amended (sandwiched) compliment during his tender teen years. The girl, whom he admired greatly, finished off their first (and last) dance with these words, "You are a wonderful dancer . . . for an awkward person." He later remarked, "It is unfair to blame Paula for my lifelong fear of dancing, but I do."

A similar experience caused him to lead his baseball team in strikeouts one season. As he went to bat, his coach told him, "Lovett, you are quite the hitter, considering it as it were." For some reason the first part of that line never did stick in young Lovett's head when he approached the batter's box that summer.

Another great example of the open-faced sandwich or the "yes, but" comes in the title of Knapp, Hopper, and Bell's article on the aspects of a compliment: "Loved Your Article, But You Missed Your Deadline."

The ultimate no-no is the club sandwich,* which is using either type of sandwich method in public.

Sandwiching is an unhealthy diet with no reinforcement value whatsoever. If you can't resist it, don't expect improved performance from your employees. In fact, you should probably expect a definite decrease in calories people will burn making efforts to improve their performance.

***B**ut . . . is a verbal eraser.*

---

* Club sandwich courtesy of Al Hauck.

III.

When People Won't Take
Your Recognition

*R*ECEIVING REINFORCEMENT, LIKE GIVING REINFORCEMENT, is also a skill. And, as with giving reinforcement, receiving it is a learned behavior. Some children spend their growing up years unable to elicit positive comments from their parents or the other adults around them. It should come as no surprise then that those people will feel awkward when someone tries to reinforce them, but receiving reinforcement well is as important as giving it.

She Was Trying,
But We Weren't Buying

I THINK EVERYONE IS FAMILIAR with the, "This old thing?" response to "I like what you're wearing." People don't realize they punish the person who tries to reinforce them if their reaction to a compliment is, "I didn't really do anything special," or, "It's my job."

A more aggressive response from some employees when their manager tries to reinforce is, "Put it in my paycheck!" This means the only thing they can conceive of as recognition is money. While it may appear hostile, a response like this indicates they have not had much social reinforcement, they don't know how to take it. They're uncomfortable and they want to stiff-arm it.

Trying to reinforce people when they don't accept it well, when they aren't able to say thank you or show some sign of acceptance, makes reinforcing even more difficult than it already is. Yet few of us can accept recognition without trying to spread the credit around to other people. Often we even use a denial statement.

When a receiver has this sort of reaction you can do one of two things. You can say, "Well, she didn't appreciate that, so I'll never do it again," thereby allowing her to punish you so much that you stop reinforcing. Or you can say, "She probably has a reason for responding that way based on her conditioning from the past."

Then whenever you notice something you think she deserves credit for, mention it to her, but keep it low key. In time she'll feel better about accepting it.

You can tell a person isn't accepting reinforcement by observing his behavior. A person may show his discomfort by breaking eye contact, shuffling, or deflecting credit to someone else. These are signals to modify your future reinforcement attempts. In the future, make sure you recognize privately as opposed to publicly, and make it a brief encounter.

Don't go on and on with a person who is visibly uncomfortable with reinforcement. A specific comment on something they did, a pat on the back, a thumbs-up sign, a wink across the room, or a smile will do. The best reinforcer in this case is something that only takes a few seconds to send and receive. Sometimes people have reinforcement thrown at them and they don't want to receive it. When this happens, the longer it takes for the encounter to be over or the bigger an audience they have increases the punishment of the encounter. Shortening the time will make receiving recognition less threatening.

Sometimes I feel more comfortable giving written, as opposed to verbal, reinforcement to certain people. It's often easier to put things on paper than saying them face-to-face.

Since our company installed a computer communications system, I notice that I receive more reinforcement from certain individuals now than I ever did when I only talked to the person over the phone or face-to-face. I also give more reinforcers. A written message is very private and the sender doesn't have to be there when I pick up my mail. Then they don't have to face the embarrassment of, "I'm reinforcing you." Also when I open my mail, I can enjoy it privately, so that my embarrassment doesn't show, or usually doesn't even occur.

Some people feel they'll never be perfect enough, that they don't deserve recognition, and never will. Don't give up on them. Just drop back a few notches on the flamboyance of your reinforcement. Turn off the bells and whistles, remove the tangibles, get rid of the audience and think about how you can make your recognition more subtle.

Jim Smith, training coordinator and PM instructor at Kodak Park, laughs about the time he and Bill Lilly, also an instructor, were becoming certified to instruct Performance Management. As they taught, I sat in the back of the room feverishly filling out feedback sheets. On the sheets I wrote comments, pointers, and things I particularly liked about their presentation skills. I made special note of gestures and exercises they should strive to repeat. When I began sharing these positive comments with them they had a hard time receiving them.

"Here we were teaching segments on receiving reinforcement, and we weren't taking it well ourselves," said Smith. "Each time Janis said something positive, we countered with, 'Well I just winged it,' or 'This is a good group.'"

Of the whole discussion Jim said, "She was trying, but we weren't buying."

The following chapters might help you recognize these reticent reinforcees. They come in all shapes and sizes. Possibly, if you learn to recognize and understand them, you can avoid having your reinforcement attempts extinguished and you can help them overcome their fear of reinforcement. You'll know to keep plugging and to keep reinforcing — even when you're trying and they aren't buying.

D*on't surrender to reticent reinforcees.*

The Undeserving
Good Soldier

SEVERAL YEARS AGO I gave Performance Management training to a group of managers in the Department of the
Army. On the second day of training I asked everyone
to write a list of things that would be reinforcing to them.
This is sometimes a difficult thing for people to do, but
they always come up with a few ideas after a momentary
struggle with writer's block.

As I walked leisurely about the room I looked to see
what people were putting on their lists. While waiting for
them to finish, I noticed that one man, a lieutenant
colonel, sat and stared at his blank reinforcer survey with
his head on his hand.

I thought, "He's not going to do this."

The room was very quiet. Everybody was working, so I walked quietly by him and continued to circle the room. I made a mental note to ask him about his list, in private, later. Well, he wasn't going to let me get by with that. When he realized I had seen his blank page he looked up and boomed, "Janis."

Everybody stopped writing and looked up.

"Yes," I said.

"I guess you noticed I haven't put anything down on this piece of paper." Then he continued, "And I'm not going to. I'm not going to fill out what my reinforcers are." At this point, to my amazement, he proceeded to bang his fist on the table to punctuate each sentence he uttered.

"If anybody asks me what my reinforcers are I won't tell them." Bam!

"If anybody tries to give me a reinforcer I won't take it." Bam!

Then he slammed his fist on the desk one last time and proclaimed, "I will NOT be reinforced!"

I sheepishly said, "Well, okay. No problem," and tried to end it there by continuing my pace around the room. (After all, he was very serious and he was a big man in a uniform.) I reasoned, "This isn't the time to discuss it, and he's going to spoil the experience for everybody."

The colonel wouldn't be dispatched. He wanted to discuss it then and there and in front of the whole brigade. "I guess you're wondering why I feel that way?" he asked.

I wasn't that curious at the moment, but he volunteered:

> When I joined Uncle Sam's Army 18 years ago, I did it to serve God and my country. I have done my best work for God and my country all these years. By your definition of reinforcement I would receive reinforcement when I have improved my performance. If I accept reinforcement for a performance this week, that would mean that I had not done my best performance last week.

So the idea of improvement, according to the colonel, represented a deficit in his performance.

I called a break.

During the break, his boss came to me and said, "Look, don't take this personally. That's just how he is. None of us are surprised. Just keep going and don't let this throw you."

Once the reinforcer list session was over, the colonel participated in the rest of the seminar. Now some people may have sat there and refused to do anything, but he was a good soldier. He did all other assignments including a very good performance improvement plan.

Two weeks later I went to do my one-on-one client follow-ups. The first appointment I had was with the colonel's boss, Mel.   As I talked to Mel he told me this story:

> The colonel gave a briefing for the general last week.   We had been under the gun for our turnaround time in getting expense checks back to people.   (This department was finance and accounting.)
>
> The colonel analyzed the problems, put a good improvement plan together and made a presentation to the general who was very impressed.   I was proud of him.   He had all the facts.   He answered all questions.   He did the right things. So after the meeting I went back to my office and wrote him a Bravo card.*

Actually, Mel didn't have any real Bravo cards.   So, he found a piece of bright yellow construction paper, folded it in half and wrote "Bravo" on the front.   Then he wrote his reinforcing remarks inside — a homemade Bravo card.   What could be better?   Mel continued the story:

> I asked the colonel to come into my office and we began chatting about the meeting.   Then I said the things to him that I had written inside the card.   I told him how well prepared I thought he was, that he had a good action plan, and told him the positive things the general said about him.   In

---

*A Bravo card is a card pre-printed with the word "Bravo." The person giving the card writes reinforcing comments about performance inside the card and gives it to the performer.

other words, I told him everything I liked about his performance. Then I handed him the Bravo card which restated those behaviors.

He just took it and read it. He didn't even look up when he finished. He just stood up abruptly without even making eye contact, almost clicked his heels, turned and walked out of my office. I thought, 'Wow, I've done something wrong now.' I knew he didn't want any reinforcement, but I couldn't help it! He had done all these good things. I realized I had offended him and felt I had better go after him and apologize.

When I got around my desk and out the door, I spotted him going down the hall headed toward the end of the building. He was stopping at every occupied office and showing off the Bravo card. I stood there and watched as he showed the card to anyone who was available. He was smiling and everybody was congratulating him. Then I realized that everything was okay.

I enjoyed hearing this story immensely. My next appointment, however, was with the colonel himself. As the time approached I became a bit nervous. Guess what was the first thing I saw perched on his desk when I walked in his office. The Bravo card. I picked it up and asked, "What is this?" He proudly gave me an explanation of what he did to earn it.

That isn't the end of the story. People have accused me of making up the ending to be dramatic. I admit it is somewhat unbelievable.

The colonel became the best performance manager there. He liked the idea of the Bravo card so much he decided to use it with his division, but he wanted it to be original. He got the print shop to give him a one-day turnaround on his design. However, his cards didn't say Bravo on the front — nothing as corny as that. They said "Wonderful." These "Wonderful" cards became his signature reinforcers and he wouldn't let anyone else use them.

I later saw these cards pinned up on cubicle walls throughout the division — the "Wonderful" cards from the colonel.

The point of this story is that the colonel believed, "Unless I'm doing my best, unless I'm perfect, don't reinforce me." For some people nothing is good enough, because, "I could have always done better." Or, in the colonel's case, "Why should I get reinforced for doing what I'm expected to do?" The colonel had trouble realizing that one can be recognized for doing a good job as well as for improvement.

Fortunately, even colonels can change.

I Feel Guilty
(Undeserving's First Cousin)

*T*HIS PERSON IS VERY CLOSELY RELATED to the "I-don't-deserve-it good soldier," with a few slight differences. I'm sure you've tried to reinforce people who said, "Oh, but I'm afraid it's not going to hold together," or, "I had such a tight deadline I may have missed something." They might say, "Well, I left out this person," or, "I hope I did it right."

Is it the American work ethic that says, "You must work all the time and never let up?" People who feel this way persistently throw in a disclaimer that more or less says, "I don't deserve that reinforcer because I didn't do enough." These same people probably felt that only straight A's were acceptable in school; that it wasn't good enough to finish college in four years. They had to graduate (with honors) in three.

These types may put up a strong front to begin with, but it is possible to break their barriers down. The important thing to remember is not to let them extinguish your behavior of positively reinforcing. Don't take it personally and thus, give up. Many people have had so little real positive reinforcement from others that they just don't know how to react at first. Rest assured, if they are human, they do want it.

Undeservers are usually some of the most deserving performers. It's a good idea to keep data on all performance, but data comes in especially handy with an "undeserving." It's difficult for a person to feel undeserving of recognition when you hold the numbers that prove they earned it right in your hand.

*D*ata speaks.

Hit And Run

ONE OF MY RECENT ATTEMPTS TO REINFORCE left me feeling like a hit-and-run victim. As soon as I tried to reinforce, the intended recipient ran over me.

I attended a seminar, one in which the participants critiqued one another's oral presentations. One man there, the owner of a national restaurant chain, was having difficulty coming across as real. His speaking personality was somewhat stiff and every time he opened his mouth, he sounded like a talking company.

By the third day, participants were still blasting him for appearing so impersonal, but I noticed some small changes he had made and wanted to recognize him for making them. I could tell he needed some reinforcement, so I said, "Gregg,* I felt you connected with the audience more this time. You made more eye contact with us and I felt closer to you." Then I went on to quote some of the things he had said that I thought added a personal touch to his presentation.

No sooner had the words left my mouth, than he looked at the back of the room, stared at the wall, and said briskly, "I've been thinking about gesturing more to put more of my personality into my presentations."

I felt cheated, and even a little stupid. Gregg had done nothing to acknowledge my reinforcer. It appeared, that while I was reinforcing him, his mind was racing ahead to the next point — how he could be better, what he would do next.

Later I told him his reaction had made me feel silly. He had barely given me enough time to say my piece, even when it was something positive about him. "From your response, which was changing the subject, it appeared you didn't hear a word I said," I told him. He didn't like hearing this, not because he cared about my opinion so much, but apparently because he'd had this type of feedback before. This trait of his caused him to come across as unfeeling and uncaring to other people as well.

Gregg was one of those people who is especially hard to reinforce. Not only does this person not receive reinforcement well, but his means of deflection is offensive because of its dismissive character.

In all probability, he simply felt embarrassed and uncomfortable with recognition. Gregg was always racing

---

Name has been changed to protect the reticent.

to the next point, which led him to be a poor listener. Being a good listener is an all-important aspect of receiving recognition.

Perhaps you recognize some of Gregg's traits in yourself. If so, be careful to at least pause when someone reinforces you and above all, listen. You may be surprised at the good things you hear.

L isten for the good news . . . and TAKE IT IN!

They Give This To Anybody

PEOPLE ARE ALWAYS AWARE, OR THINK THEY ARE, of what the guy in the next office does and doesn't do. Therefore, when tangible reinforcers, in particular, come into play, they often stir up a wave of resentment and accusations. This happens less frequently when someone receives social reinforcement. Tangibles are much more visible, so they are more likely to start the negative onslaught of "she didn't deserve it" remarks.

For example, if I saw our manager hand you a gift certificate and I know what project you were being reinforced for, I might think, "Well, I did more than she did." Or I might say to a co-worker, "She goofed off a lot. That thing just fell together, and she had more help than anybody knew about." For some reason I may feel that the amount of reinforcement you received was too much.

When this happens, the performer may slam the door on her own reinforcement. When the manager tries to recognize her, her attitude is, "Joe got such and such and I didn't agree with it, so I'm not going to have any part of this. I won't take this, because it's not good enough" or, "Even if it is good enough, I'm not going to let you win me over."

This pressure-cooker atmosphere usually starts to simmer when people compare the work they've done with the reinforcement they've received. If the work versus reinforcement ratio seems imbalanced, they may feel cheated and even deceived. If they believe the ratio doesn't measure up, they send out a loud and clear message, "I'm not playing this game, because it isn't fair."

T hank me very much.

I'm Worth More Than That

*I*F THE ONLY REINFORCERS PEOPLE GET, OR PERCEIVE THEY GET, are tangibles, when you hand them that coffee mug or that $10 gift certificate, they may ask sarcastically, "This is all it's worth for that $7 million improvement we made this year?"

When you can put a dollar value on a reinforcer, it is easy to ask, "Is this what it was worth for me to make these improvements or get this project done on time?"

A rule known as the four-to-one ratio states that a minimum of four reinforcers should be given for every one punisher (if punishers are absolutely necessary). We can apply this same ratio to social and tangible reinforcers. If people receive social reinforcement on the 4:1 ratio (a minimum of four socials to one tangible) and they receive reinforcers for behaviors, not only results, then they will view the tangible as a symbolic representation of appreciation. Then tangibles become items which serve as reminders of the social reinforcement they have already received. A tangible reinforcer carries the most impact when it symbolizes the recognized behavior or result.

The cliche, "This is something that money can't buy," is true of the good feeling that social reinforcement brings. You can't put a value on a reinforcer that makes a person feel good, one that gives a memory and one that multiplies opportunities for self-reinforcement.

R einforcement is something money can't buy.

Fear Of Greed
And Sanctimony

A FRIEND OF MINE TOLD ME after observing one of my seminars that she was impressed with the way I handled questions. To my surprise, I didn't know how to respond, even though I talk to people every day about the right way to receive recognition. I have a tendency not to accept it when I get a positive remark, because then it might appear that I agree.

I was inclined to reply, "It wasn't a difficult question" or, "It's just because I've answered that question so many times." This is a classic example of deflecting recognition by giving the responsibility for my success to someone else, or attributing it to circumstances.

I may think if I take the reinforcer I'll be participating in passive bragging, and I don't want to do that. So I have to say, "Oh, it wasn't anything." Or, "Any other consultant could have done just as well."

Sometimes we want to soften the reinforcement, even though it's positive, by passing responsibility or credit on to someone else. Many of us are trained, by our parents and by society, not to blow our own horns. We carry that to the point of not allowing someone else to praise us without correcting them. Otherwise our silence or acceptance may be seen as, "I think I'm hot stuff, don't I?"

I've learned from Brenda Jernigan, my colleague, it's okay and fun to let others know what I'm proud of, and let them help me celebrate the moment.

Every now and then, I'll walk by her office door when she's just hanging up her phone from a particularly successful phone conversation. Usually this means that she's smoothed out a rough spot for a client, found a solution to a consultant's problem, or sold something! Her silent signal is to raise her hand with a flourish, bringing the top of her hand to her lips for a loud kiss, and a smugly satisfied smile as she watches her hand float away into the air.

This is a cue for anyone around her to ask, "What is it? Tell me! What have you done now?"

Brenda helps us to know that it's time to reinforce. By stopping what we're doing and asking her for the story, we're showing our willingness to listen and join in her private celebration.

Roger Friedman, President of the New York publishing company Lebhar-Friedman, Inc., admittedly had a long way to go when he first tried to receive reinforcement. One day I told him of the many positive remarks I had been hearing about him around the organization. His employees had commented on the positive changes in his communication and management style.

Roger listened to me, then replied, "Oh you're just saying that." He immediately caught himself deflecting, however, and after a brief pause, smiled and added, "Because it's true."

Perfect.

Some of us have now stolen his phrase. We use it to catch ourselves when we're about to deflect the recognition someone tries to give.

I like to say to people: "I would rather you use 'thank you' as a response to a reinforcer, than as a reinforcer." Not that "thank you" is a bad reinforcer, but standing alone, it isn't a very personal or specific acknowledgement of what someone did for you.

Let's keep "thank you" in our receiving vocabulary. Use it when a person tries to reinforce you and you're a bit embarrassed to receive it. Force those two words out of your mouth. This will say to them, "Okay, you sent a circle and I received a circle. You tried to reinforce me and I accept."

*T*hank you, I needed that.

Denial, Guilt,
And Downright Scared

*D*ENYING THAT REINFORCEMENT IS OF ANY VALUE is a good way to resist being pulled into the process. Those who most often do this are those who don't want to feel obligated to give reinforcement to others. They have a tit-for-tat mentality — if I accept recognition, then I'm going to owe recognition.

In essence, this person is saying, "I'm not willing to give any recognition, so I better not receive it, because if I do I'm going to be in the hole. In my recognition checkbook I'll bounce checks. I don't have enough debits for all these credits."

Some people will dig in and resist when they see reinforcement happening around them. Of course, when people try to reinforce them they have to play the tough guy. In the beginning, they probably think, "Well if I just hang out here and resist long enough, it will go away just like every other management fad."

They make comments such as, "I don't believe in this. People get paid so why should we have to reinforce them?"

Even when it looks as though people are sincere with the reinforcers they are giving, as though positive things are actually coming from this "Mickey Mouse" system, the resistor types continue to dig in. Their reasoning? "If I take this and it feels good to me, then that would probably mean I should be doing this with all those people who work with me.

"First, I know I don't want to do that, and even if I wanted to, I don't have the time. So I'm going to put my head in the sand and pretend that this is not happening."

Most resistors enjoy being recognized. They've read the material about behavioral methods and recognition and their awareness is heightened. Suddenly a resistor may realize that he does need to give more reinforcers. But wait! He's been managing the way he manages (which is without positive reinforcement) for a long time. Consequently, he intellectually makes the decision, "Yes, this is the right way to treat people. I do need to recognize people more."

However, after examining his own past behavior he reasons, "If I change now, if I start reinforcing now, I'm going public with the admission that this is the right way to do it. I'm also acknowledging I've been managing the wrong way for all these years. There is no way I can ever catch up, so I'm not going to change." In the face of self-implication, he opts to "take the fifth."

One consultant had a close encounter with a "take the fifth" manager. He shared this story:

> A consultant with a manufacturing firm learned that the organization did absolutely nothing to recognize an employee's retirement. He discovered this when one night he observed an employee, a weaver, saying goodbye and shaking hands with everyone on the shift. He then put on his cap, walked to his car, and drove away. The consultant later learned that was the employee's last night on the job, after 30 years.
>
> The consultant was appalled. He went to the plant manager and said, "Hey, we need to do something here to celebrate when these people retire."
>
> The plant manager became flustered. He started wringing his hands and pacing. Then he looked at the consultant and said, "But if we do that, then they'll realize we haven't been doing it all along."

Many times people feel guilty that they haven't been giving reinforcers. They don't want to let those guilty feelings surface or to let anyone else know they feel guilty. If they ignore the whole process, they don't have to dredge those feelings up. They don't have to worry about changing, because change can be very frightening and threatening. Then they aren't forced to admit that recognition works and that they aren't comfortable with it.

They hang on to their old ways by their fingernails because they are afraid — afraid of looking someone in the eye and saying, "I like what you do." After all, "real men don't reinforce."

They are also taking the risk that their attempts will be rejected and rejection is hard stuff. Their hesitancy is totally natural. After all, for the past 20 years they've been saying to these same people, "All right, straighten up. We're into perfection around here."

*I*t *takes courage to change.*

IV.

Receiving Recognition Gracefully

*I*F YOU ARE ONE OF THOSE PEOPLE WHO HAVE A HARD TIME RECEIVING reinforcement, don't force yourself to bubble over with enthusiasm when a person reinforces you. You won't be comfortable with it and you won't come across as sincere. Allow yourself to grow into receiving recognition. To begin with, say, "Thank you."

Don't Hit A Gift Horse
In The Mouth

*T*HE MAIN THING TO AVOID when receiving reinforcement is deflecting. Some people wear what I call a recognition slicker. The slicker lets recognition run off of them like water — off onto someone else or onto the ground. When this happens, it becomes a punishing experience all around. If you are a slicker wearer, take that slicker off and absorb some of that reinforcement. Say or do something to indicate to the sender that you absorbed it. A smile is a simple way to do this, even if you smile or give eye contact for only a split second.

If you're not comfortable with it, if you can't quite force yourself to even say, "thank you," then try, "Well, I'm glad you like it." This takes the focus off you without deflecting the reinforcer.

Those singing telegrams that people try to use as reinforcers embarrass me. Once I received one. As I watched this male stripper, with a frozen smile on my face, I thought, "This is the most embarrassing experience I've ever had."

For the 20 minutes (which seemed more like hours) that the stripper was there (that half-naked man they had paid 50 bucks to sing and act lascivious), I had to stand there holding a stuffed monkey not knowing what to do with myself. I was the center of attention and I didn't know what my role was. Yet I wanted to show appreciation, because my co-workers had gone to all that trouble and expense. But, I wanted to scream, "Get him out of here!"

When I'm being reinforced or somebody tries to reinforce me, the spotlight is on me. Some people don't like to be in the spotlight. Feeling that one is in the spotlight doesn't require the presence of a crowd. Some people feel in the spotlight even in a group of two.

It's very difficult for some people to keep their mouths shut during reinforcement and let the reinforcer say those positive things. Some people may even be squelching the urge to scream out, "Will you please shut up? I can't stand all this. It's too much for me. I'm not used to it."

If you are uncomfortable with receiving reinforcement and the person giving the reinforcer is aware of your discomfort, you can always say, "Aw shucks, tweren't nothin'" and shuffle your feet. (This says to the reinforcer, "Well you know this embarrasses me, so let's laugh and break the tension.")

New York secretary Helene Levy was hesitant at first to tell her boss, Jim deGraffenreid, that he didn't really need much training in giving positive reinforcement. He was good at it already. "You know, I didn't want to sound schmaltzy, because I really meant it," she said. When she did tell him though he made her feel comfortable by looking at the floor, grinning, and saying, "Oh, shucks." They laughed.

Ray DeMoulin, General Manager of Kodak's Professional Photography Division (and a Vice President at Eastman Kodak) is praised by Pulitzer Prize winning photographers and fellow business people alike for his professional management savvy. In an interview with the *Times-Union*, in Rochester, New York, he turned the perfect phrase for receiving recognition with humor and humility. "I just get the credit because I'm the front man," he said. "But that's okay. I can handle it."

If you can do nothing else, let the person reinforcing know quickly that, "Okay, I accept it. I'm taking it in." Then move to the next subject. A smile or a brief pause are good ways to shape yourself into receiving reinforcement.

When you pause before you move onto something else, the reinforcer realizes, "He liked that."

There is always the risk that a long silence will create discomfort. However, it sends a clear signal that the reinforcer's words were meaningful and that you are taking them in.

*T*he pause that reinforces.

The Hot Potato Reinforcer

I LEARNED A GOOD LESSON ABOUT RECEIVING REINFORCEMENT from a co worker. He accepted my reinforcement and also gave some back without deflecting it or returning it to me. After he told me about how he had resolved a problem for a client, I commented, "You handled that very well." He paused for a moment, took it in, then added, "And I had a good coach."

He directed this compliment to me because we had discussed how to handle the problem ahead of time. His reply to my recognition was subtle. He could have said, "Well, it's only because I had a good coach." That statement, however, would have thrown the reinforcer back at me like a hot potato.

When he paused a minute, took it in, and then said, "And I had a good coach," rather than "But I had a good coach," he showed me that he received my recognition. I sent a circle. He received a circle. Then he sent a circle and I received it.

This may seem like pickiness over semantics, but because of his wording I felt he appreciated my reinforcer. Furthermore, I didn't feel embarrassed that I gave it. I also felt reinforced that his choice of words carried the message, "We are a team aren't we?"

You don't have to do anything that indicates you agree with the person who is reinforcing you. There is a way to receive and acknowledge reinforcement without saying, "Yes, you're right." You can say, "You're sure thoughtful to take the time to tell me that." Here, you reinforce them for reinforcing you without sending the message, "I disagree. I'm not worthy of the reinforcement."

Bill Maggard, Performance Manager of Tennessee Eastman Company's Plant Maintenance Division, told me that in addition to keeping a record of the number of reinforcers they give, the managers in his division now have a place in their logs for how many reinforcers they receive. This makes them accountable for accepting recognition and for focusing on their receiving skills as well as their giving skills. This, in turn, makes them more sensitive to the receiving patterns of those around them.

*C*atch that hot potato.

The Waiter's Survey

I conduct an ongoing experiment on unsuspecting waiters and waitresses. Whenever I go into a restaurant I try to give recognition for good service in the way of a positive comment. I've encountered deflectors, punishing deflectors, and excellent receivers of reinforcement. You might want to try this yourself. Following are my actual remarks and the responses I received:

Example 1:

Remark:	"You certainly are attentive tonight."
Reaction:	"I'm bored. I don't have anything else to do."

Example 2:

Remark:	"This is some of the best service I've ever had."
Reaction:	"It's our job."

Example 3:

Remark:	(Made after sampling the waiter's recommendation.) "You have good taste."
Reaction:	A smile, a shrug, cocked his head to one side and grinned from ear to ear.

Example 4:

Remark:	(Made after a waitress divided several entrees onto separate plates for my friend and me.) "You've really made this simple. Do you know what kind of grief we'd get if we asked most people to do this for us? You're easy."
Reaction:	A big smile and, "I'd have even done something hard for ya." Later she returned to the table and said with a big smile, "Isn't eating fun?"

Positive Moves

*I*F YOU CAN'T DO ANYTHING ELSE when somebody tries to reinforce you, smile. Don't try to rush into the next agenda item or turn and walk away. Force yourself to stop, be quiet, and for gosh sakes be still for a minute. Quit fidgeting, as Mama used to say. Even if you don't say anything, just give them eye contact or a little nod to let them know, "Yeah, I heard that." That small gesture might even be more significant than words.

Sandy starts showing her acceptance of recognitions with a smile. Her body language lets me know she enjoys recognition. Then she'll say, "We make a good team, Slick." She makes me feel like part of a team. Her remark includes me without deflecting my reinforcer. Adding a nickname or something playful that gives us both the message, "Okay we can lighten up, now. We don't have to cry, hug, or break into a rendition of "Auld Lang Syne."

Body language can say it all without saying a word.

L et's get physical.

Spread It Around

PEOPLE DEFLECT RECOGNITION without being aware of it in the name of trying to make sure their co-workers receive deserved credit. For example, I once said to the editor of our magazine, "I like the way this issue of the magazine looks."

She answered, "Well it's the first time we've done all the graphics in-house. So our graphics person is the one who did it." Sounds innocent enough, but that's a deflecting remark. After all, she had played an important role in the decisions about the look of the magazine. She didn't take credit for her contribution, however. This is not to imply that one should take credit for another's work. But a thank you as an acknowledgement of receiving reinforcement followed by information on others who deserve recognition will usually be appreciated by the person who is trying to give credit where credit is due.

She could have made it reinforcing to me to reinforce her by responding, "Oh I'm glad you liked it."

Then to be sure I know who else made a contribution she can say, "By the way this is the first issue for which we've done all the graphics in-house. I didn't know if you knew that ." That prompts me to go in and reinforce our graphic artist if I didn't already know to do so. This shows she is willing to share credit with the team, and also take some of the recognition for herself.

She can make a mental note, "Janis needs to know that this is a team effort. Let me figure out a way to let her know about that later, because I don't want to take all the credit."

If it's just too difficult to resist giving credit to someone else right then and there, she could pause long enough to say, "Well, I'm glad to know you liked that article." Then she can add, "I'm glad you liked the layout, too. You know our graphic artist does that."

Put a period on the end of the sentence that you use to take in the reinforcement. Then, go in and talk about what other people did. Anything you can do to separate the two shows your acceptance rather than your deflection.

*T*ake it in.

V.

Putting It All Together

WITH ALL OF THE DIFFICULTIES AND INTRICACIES we've identified in giving and receiving recognition, how can it ever work just right?

Don't give up yet.

Thanks For The Thanks

I KEEP MY WRITTEN MOMENTOS at home in round decorative hat boxes. A few months ago as I rummaged through them, I ran across a couple of notes I received some time ago. One was from my mentor in a previous job at Milliken & Company, Mike Georgion. Mike was a great manager and someone I continue to maintain a friendship with. On the occasion of my promotion, he wrote me a letter saying why he thought I deserved it. It was handwritten and not even on company stationery, a personal touch. So I saved it. Another was a note from Mike McCarthy, a colleague. Several years ago he wrote me a reinforcing note about my work with performance teams.

As I read over the notes I thought, "Boy, this feels so good. I bet neither one of these people could dredge up the memory of sending me these letters." That gave me an idea. I took the letters to the office, made copies, and clipped a note to each one that said, "I ran across this note the other day. I had to sit down and reread it. It still means a lot to me. See what a great reinforcer you were even five years ago?"

You can go to a person later (even later in the same day) and say, "You know it meant a lot to me for you to take time to come out there where I was working and say something positive to me."

A response, some obvious appreciation at the time someone reinforces you is good. However, if you can't reinforce the giver just yet, at least restrain yourself from punishing or deflecting. Later, if you can, come back to make the effort. You may feel that reinforcing the reinforcer later would appear perfunctory, but if you mean it, your thanks will hit the mark.

One of my colleagues sent me a note through computer mail which was a perfect reinforcer for reinforcing him. I had complimented him on the improvements he made in our performance measurement system. He responded with the following note which took in my praise, then warmed my heart back:

Reinforcing The Reinforcer

Thu 15-Mar-90 10:37pm
I noted
To   Joe Oakley
Subject   supermatrix

Joe,
        The new consultant matrix knocked me over!
I showed it off to clients today. Having the rating
scales attached is great, and I like the several
spaces you have for personalizing and options.
Nice Work.

Janis

Fri 16-Mar-90 7:53am
Joe Oakley (joakley) commented
To   Janis Allen (JAllen)
From   supermatrix

Thanks for the words of encourgement Janis. I
value your opinion and this means a lot...Joe.

*C*omputers _can_ be warm.

Who And What
Do I Reinforce?

*I*N AN IDEAL SET-UP EVERYONE REINFORCES THEIR PEERS and the person or persons who report directly to them. Those with no direct reports reinforce peers and supervisors. However, if somebody has something to celebrate who is downline a few levels from you, don't surmise that you shouldn't get involved.

If the staff of one of your direct reports has a celebration, call that direct report and say, "Nancy, I noticed your section did this and that. Good job of leading the team. I'm happy about this. Is there anything you want me to do to get involved, to give them some attention for it?"

Then if Nancy thinks it would be a good idea for you to do some reinforcing, make sure you take Nancy with you when you go. Include her in the loop of giving reinforcement. Remember to include some reinforcers for Nancy, too.

Aubrey Daniels constantly warns, "Be careful what [behavior] you reinforce because you will get more of it." Often we unconsciously reinforce behaviors that we don't want more of, then scratch our heads and wonder why that behavior continues and even strengthens. A client provided a perfect example when he told this story:

> I found that I do reinforce some behaviors I don't want more of. For example, my son spends too much time on computers. I suddenly realized that while I tell him he should spend more time doing other activities, I reinforce him much more for spending time on the computer. It struck me the other day that every time I introduce him to someone I call him "my computer wizard."

You can make some enlightening discoveries about what you reinforce at work and at home if you go back in time and examine what happened to a person in the past when he exhibited a certain behavior. If he continues an unwanted behavior, you may be subtly reinforcing him.

In order to uncover the "hidden" reinforcers when examining past occurrences you must be honest with yourself about what did happen as opposed to what should have happened.

*Be careful what you reinforce;
you will get more of it.*

Mean What You Say

ONE OF THE FIRST THINGS YOU MAY RUN INTO when you make a change in your style is that people will doubt your sincerity. They will suspect that this new positive approach is yet another "fad du jour."

One man who refused to go along with "all this positive malarkey" remarked to a consultant, "I was here before you got here and I'll be here when you leave!"

Those managers who have tried different things know that seasoned employees will play the wait-and-see game when it comes to anything new. Positive reinforcement is geared toward approaching a person and saying something like, "I'm pleased with the way you handled that." This sets the novice reinforcer up for some initial rejection and embarrassment. But look at it from the receiver's point of view.

If I say this to a co-worker and I've never said anything like this to him before, even though I've been working with him for 15 years, what will his reaction be? Suspicion.

Your sincerity may be viewed skeptically not because you're doing something wrong, but because you've got 5, 10, or 15 years of history to overcome. The conditioning over time that employees in certain environments have is, "If you see the manager coming, look out."

When I train non-managers, one of the main issues they want to resolve is, "How do I know this is sincere?" They make remarks such as, "That manager just completed training. That's the only reason he's doing this."

They're right. People usually complete training and emerge enthusiastic and ready to start. They have a genuine, sincere interest in reinforcing. Then, their employees respond with, "Don't do this to me."

Years ago, I worked with a manager named Alex. On the second day of the training session he said, "You know, Janis, you talk about those managers who never contact anybody unless they have bad news to deliver, they want to beat up on them for something, or they want to give them extra work. I just realized, sitting here in class this morning, that I'm one of those managers. If I make the effort to talk to somebody or call them on the phone, that's what it's all about. I realize I've got to change.

We talked it over. The next morning he came in and said, "I tried to reinforce and, oh boy, what a horrible experience."

He had returned to his office and discovered that his secretary, Lisa, had voluntarily taken on and completed a rather time-consuming project. Although he had mentioned the project to Lisa, he didn't ask her to do it. Yet she had taken the initiative to crunch the numbers, separate the information for each supervisor, and write a cover letter for his approval and signature. She had saved him many hours of work.

Alex picked up the letter, marched to Lisa's desk and said, "I just saw this report you wrote and this letter is excellent. You have saved me considerable time here and I appreciate it. I didn't know you knew precisely what I wanted, but this is exactly how I would have done it. This is great!"

Lisa's reaction? A blank stare.

The silence finally became unbearable for Alex, so he turned quickly to run to the safety of his office. As he started to duck through the door Lisa said, "Alex, what did you really come out here for?"

This was Lisa's honest reaction. She wasn't trying to punish Alex, but she did. He received a negative consequence for his attempts at positive reinforcement. What is Alex's rate of reinforcing likely to be in the future?

People go out on a limb, try some positive reinforcement, and when they don't get the kind of reaction they expected, conclude, "This recognition stuff is for the birds." What Alex, or anyone in his predicament, must keep in mind is that it will take time for their employees to learn how to respond appropriately to recognition if they have no history of it. It will take Lisa some time to believe that Alex means what he says. That is only natural.

Alex must come back again, and again, and again, being specific and positive, just as he once came back again, and again, and again being specific and negative.

Of course we might take pity on poor Alex, take Lisa aside and tell her not to have this disbelieving reaction. This isn't particularly fair, because her reaction is honest and she knows more about her own positive reinforcers than Alex does.

If you have a history of negative management, expect this reaction. Then deal with it with patience and persistence. Another suggestion: Keep data on performance. It's difficult to be insincere, or perceived as such, if you refer to the data.

For people to perceive you as sincere, you must have a clear intention with no hidden agenda. Some managers make the mistake of trying to package something they want the person to have (such as a seminar for improving organization skills) as a reinforcer. This, "I'll-kill-two-birds-with-one-stone ploy," is readily transparent to the recipient. If you want an employee to develop certain skills don't attempt to dress it up in a "reinforcer" Halloween costume. That's trickery, not treatery.*

If an employee lists seminars or training, etc. on his reinforcer list, then this type of reinforcer is acceptable.

Nancy Scott, with Eastman Kodak, said, "I always tell people to be patient and gentle on those who have seldom given reinforcement, but are now trying. Their efforts at recognition should be reinforced. Improvement in their delivery of reinforcement will come with practice."

When people finally realize you intend for positive recognition to be an ongoing effort, they do come around. They accept it when they believe it is a sincere effort to show appreciation to people for their contributions. Then they start trying to find ways they can reinforce others. When they can reinforce both their peers and their managers, that's when they feel they are in the driver's seat.

The reinforcer has to be theirs, not yours.

Say What You Mean

*L*ET PEOPLE KNOW EXACTLY WHAT BEHAVIOR THEY DID or result they achieved that you are trying to reinforce. Some organizations with recognition systems rely exclusively on group goal setting and celebrations for reinforcement. Some are quite successful again and again at setting a goal, getting the group together, improving quality 95 percent, and then celebrating. Bring in the pizza. Well, this is fine, but not if it's the only type of recognition people receive. Meet a goal, celebrate, meet a goal, celebrate. Pizza, pizza, pizza!

Nothing is wrong with a pizza, a party, a celebration for reinforcing groups of people who achieve a goal. To make your reinforcement efforts stronger, though, you must reinforce the specific performance of individuals. When people pull together and operate as a team to achieve, you must use a combination of individual recognition and group reinforcers.

When you reinforce a team effort there is always at least one person, sometimes several, who worked smart, worked hard, and put in an extra effort to make the team project successful. Those on the other end of the spectrum will be the people who didn't do much to pull their load and let others carry them along. Some may have even disagreed with the project or the goal and created obstacles that the others had to overcome.

When we only recognize the group, recognition isn't distributed according to how it was earned. We can't completely balance the scales, but there are some things we can do to make them stand a little more evenly. When you give the individuals in a group the same reinforcer, you are trying to reinforce teamwork. While doing so, try not to punish your best people. They know who they are. Almost invariably, the people who know they carried the team harbor some resentment.

These people want the manager or supervisor to acknowledge their extra contributions. A manager doesn't have to do this in public. Identify the person or persons who deserve extra credit. Go to them privately, preferably ahead of time, and say, "I want to let you know I saw what you did on that project team. I know if not for your efforts we might not have met this goal." Try to be as specific as possible about their particular contribution. For example, "I noticed you picked up somebody else's load when he failed to collect the data."

Don't create a winners-losers competition. Simply recognize and appreciate the individual's willingness to go all out. When you tell him this prior to the celebration, he is usually much more willing to go and enjoy the party with everyone else.

Remember the times you have gone to a lot of trouble and effort to make something successful. You put in the midnight oil and smoothed out problems your manager never knew about. What if your manager did find out what you did and told you about it? What if he said, "I don't know how you pulled this off. Tell me how you did it." Wouldn't hearing that be as valuable to you as a pizza?

An old horror movie title comes to mind: *I Know Who You Are And I Saw What You Did.* What most people want to know (in a positive way) is that their manager, co-worker, supervisor, or team leader knows who they are and sees what they do.

I saw what you did and I know who you are.

Now And Later

R EINFORCE DESIRABLE BEHAVIORS AS SOON AS POSSIBLE. Randy
Cooper, Department Manager of Color Sensitizing and
Color Paper Manufacturing, shared a story:

> I was an engineering supervisor in one of our
> company's departments back in 1985. One night
> an electrical power interruption caused the
> computers to go down. At the time these were
> getting to be fairly old computers and starting
> them up after losing power was tricky.

> The engineering, maintenance and operation
> people put in some long, hard extra hours. The
> results, though, were good. They restored the
> computers and got the equipment back on line.

They made what could have been a very difficult recovery and made it almost transparent. They all had a real feeling of accomplishment and comraderie the following morning.

I made a point to try and personally contact the nine individuals who made the recovery happen. I caught all but one man. It wasn't for lack of trying, but our paths never seemed to cross.

About two days later I finally ran into him in the stairwell. None of the spirit and teamwork that had been present with the other eight was here with this man two days later. Because of the timing it was obvious to me that my words had practically no meaning to him.

There was no less enthusiasm on my part, but the timing just didn't seem to fit. The non-verbal reading I got from him was that it was a flat kind of interaction. This left an impression on me.

If you can't do it quickly, recognition should take on a different form. You need to try to recapture the moment, by asking the person to talk to you about the past event.

Randy learned a valuable lesson about the importance of immediate reinforcement. Immediately after or during the behavior is always the preferred time to reinforce. Still, if this isn't possible don't make the mistake of saying, "I just heard what Joe did while I was away on vacation, but that was a week ago and if I say anything now it won't be immediate enough. I'll talk to him about it when I give him his performance appraisal."

Wrong.

Talk to the person anyway and get him to talk to you.

My Mama always told me, "Better late than never." Well, reinforcement is better if you give it during the behavior, but it's still better late than never.

Of course, you have plenty of opportunities to catch people in the act, which is the best time to reinforce. You don't have to produce a tangible or hire a band. You can weave rich seams of recognition into a single conversation. It doesn't take much.

Try for now, but better late than never.

Reprinted by permission of UFS, Inc.

The Need For Speed

SOCIAL REINFORCERS DON'T HAVE TO BE SPOKEN WORDS. For example, if someone says something in a meeting that you think is an astute comment you don't have to stand up and cheer, or shout, "Amen!" You can support and encourage someone subtly and silently with body language, especially when you know he is nervous about making a presentation. You can lean slightly toward him, nod when he makes a point, and smile. Keep your eyes on the person for a second or two after he speaks, so he knows you are interested.

When a person isn't confident of their participation, or how they are coming across to the new manager, these minor moves in even one member of the audience can pull them through. After the presentation, catch their attention as soon as you can and make eye contact. Give them a wink or a subtle thumbs-up.

When walking by someone who is working or whom you've just had a positive interchange with, throw up your hand. Show your approval. Laughing when somebody says something he hopes is funny can be a life saver. Laughter itself is reinforcing to people. Most people love to say things to make other people laugh. And, as author Robert Fulghum says, "Laughers are holy people."

One of the reasons Aubrey Daniels is reinforcing to be around is that he laughs easily and genuinely. His neighbor once said to him, "Aubrey, I just love to talk to you because you'll laugh at anything." Of course, Aubrey thought that remark was rather funny, too.

One thing I like about my job is our informal office environment. Sometimes when I have just gotten off the phone with a client and we have talked about a success or someone has received the go-ahead to get started with a consulting contract, I run out into the open office making unintelligible noises.

If I notice that Brenda or Aubrey (my closest office neighbors) are on the phone, I silently hop around in front of their doors until it's safe to make loud noises.

When they finally ask me what all the excitement is about, I grin smugly and say nothing, but keep hopping. They play along and beg me to tell them. When I finally reveal my secret, Brenda squeals and Aubrey stops whatever he's doing and says, "Well tell me about it." Then Tracy comes in, listens to the story, gives me a hug and says, "I'm so proud of you!" When Alice hears the news, she remarks, "Well, ya done good." And Joseph makes me a paper hat. Satisfied now, I return to my office. I have a tiger in my tank.

R einforce the moment.

Listen For The Value

Ever notice the words people use when they give positive reinforcement? Often, their metaphors reveal what they value.

Dominic Del Rosso, Maintenance Supervisor at Lebhar-Friedman Publishing, found this to be true when he attended a Performance Management staff meeting headed by his manager Jim Granato, Chief Financial Officer.

Del Rosso had never met with this group before, but took time from his schedule to attend, even though it meant he had to do the presentation in his work clothes before a roomful of others dressed in suits. He sat before the group and shared his plans for reducing expenses, changing the current distribution system, and investigating inventory changes.

Impressed with Del Rosso's initiative, Granato exclaimed, "That'll get the cash register ringing!" This remark conveyed the high value he placed on Del Rosso's ideas and consequently his words proved very reinforcing.

Later that afternoon when I spoke with Del Rosso about his presentation he smiled and said, "That was a pretty good meeting. I enjoyed it."

Enjoy meetings? How often do those two words appear in the same sentence?

On A Positive Note

MANY PEOPLE TELL ME they have been taught not to write while another person is talking. They say this is especially true if the speaker is an employee, because he may be suspicious about what is being written. He may be concerned you are writing something, possibly something negative, to go in his file. Well, this is a valid point. You should make sure the speaker is viewing your note-taking in the right light.

Realistically though, if you are attending a presentation and writing down specific points the speaker makes, it's apparent you are not writing a letter to your mother. Your eye contact and the times you choose to write demonstrate that you are tuned in to what he is saying. You are participating by taking notes. This type of note-taking reinforces the presenter. He sees that his words are important enough to make you push your pencil.

You can use this same method when in a conversation with an individual. If he is relating information that you think is important, you can say, "Look, I don't want to forget these things. Do you mind if I take some notes?"

In the consulting and training profession we often ask for written comments about our presentations. I sometimes take the positive remarks about a speaker and make a collage of them by gluing them onto a piece of colored paper. Jane Sparks helps me with this, then puts them in a plastic three-hole punch cover and we send them to the speaker.

Everyone who has received one of these has told me they enjoy them. Most of them carry the collage when they're traveling and reread it once in awhile. Reading a few positive comments about yourself can be inspirational, especially before you make a presentation. A sheet like this can also serve as a pick-me-up on those down days. Let's face it, we all have a few of those. Referring to something like this is also a good step toward self-reinforcement. After a while you can remember those positive comments and retrieve them whenever you feel the need.

Positive written comments have a "this-is-your-life" effect. You may not work with many public speakers, but this is an easily adaptable process. You can easily compile a list of positive comments you hear about a presentation — positive gossip in writing. Or you can put together several reports about the quality in a person's department. Clip out the quality performance numbers for this week, the next week, and the next, and add a comment with a magic marker such as, "You did it!" (Hint: Using color always helps in any potential reinforcer.) One person even slipped me a positive comment written on a pink paper dinner napkin. I still have it.

Writing down all ideas in a brainstorming session with a group of people reinforces sharing ideas and encourages participation. In these sessions one person writes all ideas on the flip chart. It is very important to write down all suggestions. When a person makes a statement, they can see their words formed up there on the sheet of paper. For a few brief moments they become immortalized. Sound silly? How many times have you caught yourself reading your suggestion over and over when it's up there "in lights?"

We tried this theory with one group of seminar participants. During several days of training I asked each of them to compose several questions and answers about quality reinforcement techniques. Later I transferred the questions, which were very good, on to yellow flash cards to use in future sessions. Next to each question and answer was printed the name of the person who submitted it. Later, on a return session with the group, I gave each of them a package of the cards. Most of the group were in high-ranking supervisory or management positions with their organization. They had a ball going over the cards and finding their names.

Knowing that someone else considers your words important enough to write lends a certain credibility to your image as a unique and creative individual.

Words can be written into someone's head as well.

For instance, my client Harry Estes, once introduced me by saying to a group of managers at the beginning of a meeting ". . . And I know you'll have a good time today, because if you can't have a good time with Janis Allen, you can't have a good time."

Whenever I have a tough time with a group, I repeat Harry's comments to myself and then I knock 'em dead.

Give someone's words to them
as a souvenir.

To-Do It Now

*I*T'S EASY TO SAY, "When I have the time I'm going to come back and let that person know I saw what she did and I liked it." Of course, you lose immediacy when you wait too long. Another problem is, the longer you procrastinate, the more likely you are to forget it entirely.

If possible, recognize it as soon as you think about it. If you can't do that for some reason, at least write a reminder on your to-do list. Otherwise, you diminish the chances you will ever think of it again.

How many times have you ever received excellent service on an airline, at a department store, or at your bank? At the time you may have thought, "I should write a letter about that." Chances are, even those of us with the best of intentions never get around to doing it. We complain about the poor quality of service in our country today. We're tired of surly waiters, inattentive clerks, snobbish customer "service" personnel. Often we get so fed up with rude treatment we ask to speak to a manager and tell her about a particularly obnoxious employee.

Compare the number of times you've complained to the number of times you've said, "That John Jones over there just gave me such excellent advice and service I wanted to tell you about it."

The only thing that ensures I'll follow through with my intentions is if I do it on the spot or write a note reminding myself to send a note later. If something makes it to my list of things to do, usually I'll do it. This works for me because not only am I now faced with an "official" reminder, I also find it reinforcing to check things off my list when I complete them.

It can be reinforcing to reinforce.

A Card Cache

ONE THING THAT DETERS SOME OF US from giving reinforcement, other than verbal, is the lack of time and memory.
We think, "I need to go out and get a card so I can write
that note." Then we forget, or never find the time.
Finally, we decide it's too late and assure ourselves, "I'll
catch it next time."

Cards are easy. Also, they are almost universal reinforcers. If you keep a supply on hand, you are more
likely to write a note.

Many people use formalized memos and letters of
commendation to reinforce. Those are fine. Frequently
though, people are reluctant to use them. They aren't
quite sure of the company's policy and they also worry,
"If I put this in a person's file, what will I do when

appraisal time rolls around? Can they use it as leverage?" Their performance could have changed by then.

Generally, people have good intentions and want to reinforce, but they are a little afraid. They might not be able to follow through with the appraisal rating or the money. Someone might tell them to put their money where their mouth is. The more casual reinforcers, like a few positive words on a little message card, may prove less threatening. These casual notes put the focus on the individual's behavior *this week*, not on his overall performance. Reinforcer cards can also be humorous if you are well-attuned to the receiver's funny bone.

People are more likely to display cards than they are to tack up a whole formalized memo. They then get even more reinforcement when friends and co-workers stop by and read the message. When you send a card to someone, you're probably not going to send a photocopy of it to a large distribution, as you often feel compelled to do with formalized letters. It is more sincere, more personal. With a card, the receiver knows you are not trying to impress people with how you recognize others. It's from you to the receiver and he chooses whether to display it.

Having a few cards in your desk drawer or somewhere on hand helps you recognize more often. You can do it instantly and you don't have to go shopping.

*W*hen you want to send the very best.

Paper Laughter

*G*IVING CARTOONS AS REINFORCERS is an inexpensive, fun and personal way to recognize something. I clip out cartoons, some that remind me of specific individuals, and keep them in a file folder. Then when I want to recognize someone, I tape or staple that cartoon onto a piece of my notepaper and write a comment about whatever I want to reinforce. The behavior or result that I'm recognizing doesn't have to tie in with the cartoon. I can cover that association with my written remarks.

My favorite business cartoons are in *USA Today* and the *New Yorker,* but cartoons are in almost every publication. Today many cartoons use a person's name such as Millie or David or Joe. This practice is also popular with greeting cards. Of course, you don't have to send the card to a person with that name, but often, if I see a card that has the first name of somebody I know on it, I buy it and save it until it's time.

You can do the same thing with a strip cartoon. If you see one about a person who is a computer junkie and you know a computer whiz, clip it out. Then, when it's time to send that person a note, tape the strip to it. Sharing a laugh is another universal way to reinforce.

*H*e *who laughs, lasts.*
        —*Mary Pettibone Poole*

Getting Personal

T HE MOST COMMON MISTAKE PEOPLE MAKE in delivering reinforcement is associated with personalizing it for the
person who has earned it. People often make the
mistake of delivering something to another person that
they themselves would want. I might think that everyone likes public recognition since I like it. I enjoy
reporting to my peers about my work. Therefore,
because I enjoy it, I say, "Jim come on up here and tell
us all about it." For poor Jim this may be the equivalent
of public humiliation.

In 1986 a poll was taken of American adults — men
and women from different cities and across all cultural
and economic strata. One of the questions was, "What
do you fear most?" In a forced ranking of one to ten,
Americans said they feared public speaking the most,

193

followed by death (probably a fate they fear is the direct result of public speaking).

Public speaking would have been on the bottom of my list. I wouldn't be doing what I do for a living if public speaking were my number one fear. However, even though so many people hate it, time and again, especially with team projects, we give this as a "reinforcer." "Okay, we're going to have the team go to the corporate office and make a presentation about what they're doing."

I know from experience that the team then spends weeks getting ready for these things. Some are reinforced by it. Many are not. Maybe two or three will enjoy the experience. The others plan to call in sick.

A reinforcer listed by people at all levels is, "Talk to me about a project. Ask me how I accomplished a goal."

An operator told this story:

> I told my supervisor about an idea for improving the quality of our product. The supervisor said, "We don't pay you to think around here. When you come to this plant, leave your brains in the car. We don't need them."

> I told that supervisor, "I can't do that. I have a compact car."

It's painful to have your opinion ignored. When someone ignores your suggestions, it somehow negates your validity as a valuable, thinking person. The only sacrifice you have to make, when you ask a good performer her opinion or advice, is a small amount of your time. If you are a good listener, you might just learn something as well.

One of my colleagues told me about an experience he had receiving reinforcement through our electronic mail. The story relates the necessity of a personal tone in getting recognition across to the receiver.

He wanted to report some good news, so he sent the information to persons A and B on the computer communications system. He told me that he was reading his mail later, and happened to get responses from A and B at the same time.

He said, "I just wanted to tell you about how differently reinforcement feels depending on how one words it." Person A had answered his message in this way. "Thank you for keeping me informed." Person B's reply said, "You have resurrected the dead. You're amazin'." A very big difference in messages and feeling. According to him, one message was positively reinforcing; the other wasn't. There is a huge difference between saying "Thank you" and giving positive reinforcement or recognition.

Person A's message focused on himself. Person B's message focuses on the sender's performance. A's message is better than nothing, but only slightly. It is cold and distant. Its real message is: "I acknowledge that you have done this," rather than, "I'm going to make a positive value judgement about how good you are." Some people try to reinforce this way because it's about as warm as they can get.

Steve Smith of Tennessee Eastman sends "puzzle notes" as reinforcers. An example at the end of this section is a note he sent to a colleague thanking him for his own reinforcing behaviors.

Steve sends these personalized, humorous, and fun notes to quite a few people as reinforcers. Who wouldn't enjoy one? I imagine that most people save these notes for a long time, and may put them on display. It's obvious to the receiver that Steve has put a lot of himself into these recognition notes.

Peggy Noonan, former President Reagan's speech writer, in her book, *What I Saw at the Revolution*, tells about a personal note she received from the president. She had been writing for the president for four months and had not yet even met him. One day the president wrote two simple words, "Very Good," on one of her speech drafts. She said:

> I stared at it. Then I took a pair of scissors and cut it off and taped it to my blouse, like a second-grader with a star. All day people would notice it and look at me; I would beam back in a quietly idiotic manner.

With most reinforcers, the best way to find if a performer will be reinforced is to ask. The only way to know if Barry wants his name in the company newsletter is to ask Barry. Any time that you attempt to use one type of reinforcer, like baseball caps, with everyone, you're going to hit some and you're going to miss some. Even if the majority says, "I want a baseball cap," that minority who didn't want a baseball cap isn't going to feel reinforced.

Some people love having their names and pictures displayed on bulletin boards when they accomplish something. Others will run you out of town if you try to do that. Reinforcer preferences differ with region, gender, social status, and of course, age. For example, younger employees tend to want more time off than older ones. So, ask people what they like. Have your peers, managers and direct reports fill out reinforcer lists. (We sometimes call them reinforcer surveys.) Keep the lists in a loose-leaf book, but only after obtaining each person's permission to do so. Then keep the book readily accessible to everyone.

Another way to personalize any reinforcer is to use the person's first name when delivering it. Then tell him why the behavior or result you are reinforcing is important to you.

We haven't done any definitive studies of cultural differences in reinforcer preferences, but of course they exist. Some of our consultants encountered this when working with PPG Industries, Inc. While working in England, we quickly found that some of our friends in the United Kingdom found several U. S. tangible reinforcers rather strange. "Baseball caps?" they asked.

PPG hosted a seminar for several of its engineers from the Taiwanese manufacturing organization, Nan Ya Plastics. Jack Weller informed us of the most personal reinforcer the Taiwanese can give. Since their work week lasts six days, Sunday is known as a day to spend with family. Hence, a person feels great honor if asked to spend time with a co-worker and his family on Sunday.

Blanket reinforcers don't exist. I hate to be the one to give you that news, because it is so much easier to organize a company picnic and invite 500 people. "Bring the family. We met a goal." Or you can hand out 10,000 coffee mugs with the company logo printed on them. That's easy. The hard part is reinforcing people one by one. This is up to the employees' direct supervision, not up to the person at the head of the organization, although he or she can be a part of it.

By now you may be getting the idea that this reinforcement stuff is tough. You're right.

However, if you take the time to individualize and personalize, you'll make a profitable impression. When people know you recognize what they do, because you take the time to tell them, they'll put their best efforts toward doing a good job for you.

*O*ne half of the world cannot understand the pleasures of
the other.
—*Jane Austen*

From: U831547 - - ECDVM1   Date and time   05/23/89 14:11:13
To: U830754 - - ECDVM1   COOPER GEORGE F

From: Mike Warner, Plant Maintenance Division, B-T500, 4906

Subject: MWS PROGRESS
George and CREW 4325;

    Thanks for coming to the team management consultants team meeting Thursday afternoon and updating us on the progress of your team. It was encouraging to us to hear the first hand account of "how it is going" from someone who is implementing this new style of management. We know that it has taken a lot of extra effort and willingness to change, not only from you but also from your crew. You all have not only identified the tasks that can be transferred but have started transferring them. You have already started documenting the process of executing many of these tasks and accepting the responsibility for training others in how to do these tasks. To say that you are making good progress is an understatement. CREW 4325 and George Cooper you are to be commended for a truly outstanding effort and example of how a team can manage its own business. If there is any way that any of the team management consultants can assist you please let us know.

cc: ATEAM   J. M. Warner

A LOT OF PEOPLE THINK RATING IS ⬤, AND THAT MIKE WARNER IS A 🐷,

BUT IN A 🌐 WHERE NO ONE BELIEVES IN SAYING THANK YOU, MIKE

WARNER STANDS ⚥ 🕺💃. THANKS MIKE FOR TAKING THE 🕐 TO MAKE WORK 🎨.

Reading Steve Smith's puzzle notes is reinforcing even if the positive comments aren't directed your way. (Note: The pig is called a "suckbog," an inside joke with the group. A suckbog is the equivalent of a "yes man.")

           — Steve

Be a Snoop – Premack

*D*R. DAVID PREMACK FORMALIZED THE PREMACK PRINCIPLE, although it was truly invented by Grandma, ("Eat your vegetables and you can have dessert."). Premack discovered that "a behavior which occurs frequently can be used to re-inforce a less frequent, but desired behavior." The Premack Principle involves observing what people do when given a choice. Whatever they choose tends to be a reinforcer. Then a contingency can be arranged be-tween something that needs to be done and the choice activity.

In other words, "If you do this first, then you can do that." It's like playing, "Let's Make A Deal." We can and often do play this little game with ourselves.

You can easily learn the Premack reinforcers of family members, peers, friends and employees by taking the time to listen and observe closely. A good exercise is to choose someone and observe what they do and talk about when they have a choice. Be a detective. Observe what they like to do, what they laugh at, what they eat at break time, what they talk about, what they doodle when they take notes.

Premack is an especially valuable tool to use at work. You may observe that a mechanic, when given the choice, works on electric motors as opposed to pumps. Or you may notice that an assistant, when given the choice, prefers filing over typing. You can use these observations to strengthen the typing behavior. For example, "After you finish typing these memos, will you help me with my filing?"

You can also use Premack reinforcers with your family. Often, if you observe closely, you will find out about hobbies, interests, preferences in movies and books — details you never would have guessed about certain individuals. Some work-related behaviors people enjoy are involvement with strategic planning, developing plans, getting feedback, making presentations, and hearing about project status. If an employee enjoys being in on culture change activities or problem-solving teams, use those two activities as reinforcers for another behavior you'd like to occur more often.

You may know a few of an individual's reinforcers because you've worked with them for a long time. When you consciously observe, however, you may be surprised how many reinforcers you weren't previously aware of, even if you thought you knew the person well. Ironically, the closer we are to people the more we tend to overlook their everyday activities, likes, and dislikes.

One father discovered a very powerful Premack for his 16-year-old son. He allowed his son to drive the family car to school *if* he completed chores around the house. "I can get him to do anything," he said.

Another father said, "I've found with my children, if I can associate the Premack reinforcer with the things they usually consider drudgery, they soon become caught up in the drudgery event."

*M*ake some activities contingent, not free.

Becoming A Self-Reinforcer

*T*HE IMMEDIACY CRITERION PRESENTS A GOOD ARGUMENT for self-reinforcement. When you can reinforce yourself by taking pride in the things you do, you meet that criterion. You learn to pat yourself on the back for every step of the way toward a goal. You can pause and feel that satisfaction even before anyone else knows you've done it. When it comes to immediacy, you can't beat self-reinforcement.

It's one thing to talk about receiving reinforcement well and becoming self-reinforcing, but it's another thing to practice it. Being a good reinforcee is enjoyable, but it isn't always easy. I often catch myself doing exactly the opposite of what I tell others to do. One example in particular stands out in my mind.

I had just completed a particularly satisfying session with a group of top-notch clients. They were such a positive and enthusiastic group that when we completed our two-day seminar I felt I was leaving old friends behind. I had decided to drive the distance from Atlanta to this beautiful mountainous area of Tennessee so I could enjoy the scenery. Since I knew I'd be in the car for many hours, I diligently supplied myself with a load of well-intentioned, I'm-going-to-be-productive items.

Of course I brought along some music tapes, but I also brought tapes for dictation, and some Portuguese language tapes. At the time I had plans to go to Brazil on a business trip and thought I should learn a few words. Of course, I had set myself the small sub-goal of speaking fluent Portuguese by the end of my trip.

I hadn't listened to the language tapes on the trip up to Tennessee, so I planned to hone my language skills on the return trip. I planned to study Portuguese, then reinforce myself with music, study Portuguese, then listen to some more music. It would be a snap. I thought, "I'm going to be good at this."

After this very satisfying seminar, I got in the car and hit the road. I popped in the Portuguese tape. The tape buzzed on for awhile and I realized I hadn't heard a word of it. So I rewound it and told myself, "Okay let's start at the beginning." A few minutes later, I realized I still hadn't heard a word. Then I thought, "What's going on here?"

I was having so much fun thinking about the last two days, that I didn't give a pig's Latin about Portuguese. It was the first time I had experienced a quiet moment in several days. My stay in Tennessee had been a flurry of constant activity. Once in the car, the mental videotape of all the good things that had happened started running through my head. I had also collected and read the feedback sheets that the group wrote for me at the end of the session and they were positive.

Suddenly I realized, "I'm trying to do something unnatural here. I'm trying to get directly back to work. I'm pushing myself too hard."

I ejected the tape and drove the scenic stretch through the mountains in silence, allowing myself to think about the things that had happened — funny things, comments that were written, remarks people had made.

Glutton for reinforcement that I am, I kept myself amused, repeating the positive phrases to myself for quite a while.

Even after two days of talking about receiving reinforcement and how to savor the moment, I was still thinking, "Get in the car. Learn Portuguese. Work, work, work." I needed to allow myself some time to think about the successful meeting I'd just completed.

Here, the external reinforcement of a positive experience had been given to me. I now had the opportunity to internalize it. I was in the car alone. All I had to do was give myself a break and the time to enjoy it.

I am sure many of you can relate to this.

Even though driving home after work is the perfect time to review the positive things about the day, we tend to plan what we're going to do next, or worry about whatever went wrong that day. We say that people should give at least four positive reinforcers for every punisher or negative they use. The same rule applies for positive self-statements and reinforcers received.

At the end of your day take a few moments to go back and think about what happened when you first got to work that morning. Then mentally go through the day's events and try to focus on the highlights of the day. What were the things that happened when you felt you'd made a good decision? What about when someone came back to you and told you about an action they had taken on your advice? That was positive. What were the things that made you feel good? Try it. On most days I bet you'll come up with a good ratio of successes to "failures."

It's great to be able to receive reinforcement comfortably and gratefully from other people. Then there is that whole other level of reinforcing yourself. Most of the time this does not mean you must stop and do something forced like, "Okay, what do I need to reinforce myself for today?" You can take a reinforcement break in a much more natural way.

For instance, if you feel that you're at a point in a project where you could use a boost, turn to someone and say, "Look at this will you? Can you give me some comments on this report?"

I did that on the plane with a co-worker once. We had boarded the same flight from Atlanta to New York. I had designated the two hours on the plane to begin outlining a new project, and was proud of myself when I completed a big portion of it.

Instead of plunging on and working more, I took a reinforcement break. I got up from my seat, walked a few rows back to Ned and said, "Would you take a second to look at what I've done? I'm halfway through it and I'm excited about how it's coming together."

He looked at it, and made some positive comments about the value of it. When I returned to my seat, I felt good. I felt refreshed. I felt like working some more.

This is one way to get recognition from other people, but often you can do it yourself. Just give yourself a short breather and focus on the things you've done well so far. Lean back and literally take a few deep breaths and savor it.

I learned many lessons about becoming a self-reinforcer from my mother. Not long ago we were bringing her home from a week-long stay at the hospital.

I was helping her settle in when she said, "Janis, climb up there in the pantry and get the Sunday School money jar down." When I returned with the money she instructed me, "Now I want you to call the Sandy Mush Florist and have them deliver a $7.50 dish garden to me." I looked at her quizzically. "I'm the one who sends the flowers for the Sunday School class so get the money and pay for the flowers when they come."

My mother wasn't going to pass up what she deserved even if she had to send it to herself. I thought this was great.

The more self-reinforcing we are, the more reinforcement we are able to give. When we know our own
reinforcers and we use them, we are better equipped to
recognize the reinforcers of others and deliver them with
finesse.

Being able to reward yourself for the positive and pro-
ductive parts of your life is not a self-serving goal. It is
an integral element for enjoying all your endeavors that
ultimately leads to helping others enjoy theirs.

*T*ake time to savor your own little victories.

ABOUT THE AUTHORS

Janis Allen first heard about positive reinforcement when she was the Personnel Manager for a Milliken & Company manufacturing plant in 1972. Later, she became a Performance Manager at Milliken, and spent eight years training and assisting managers to implement Performance Management systems in their departments, plants, divisions and at the corporate level.

She was a consultant for Aubrey Daniels & Associates, Inc. for 10 years, and a vice president for three. Her client work included Blue Cross and Blue Shield, 3M, Xerox, Eastman Kodak, Emerson Electric, and Lebhar-Friedman Publishing. Since 1991 she has had her own consulting business based in Atlanta.

Her first book, *Performance Teams*, was published in 1982. She lives in Atlanta, Georgia, where she enjoys refurbishing and decorating her eighty-year-old house.

Gail Snyder received her journalism degree from Georgia State University. She also has technical education and experience in the printing industry. She is the editor of *Performance Management Magazine*, and a staff writer for Aubrey Daniels & Associates, Inc. Her articles are being used as examples of excellent writing on a scientific subject to teach graduate students who are interested in publishing their work.

Gail, her husband Jack, their three-year-old son David, and their two dogs Muggs and Domino, reside in bucolic bliss in the country county of Cherokee, Georgia.

ABOUT THE BOOK: GAIL'S STORY

When I first started writing this book with Janis, I already knew she was a positive, enthusiastic, and upbeat person. Janis is one of those rare individuals who practices what she preaches. I found this out through personal experience because she used her positive recognition techniques on me every step of the way. I knew what she was doing and so did she, but that didn't do a thing to diminish the power of her reinforcers.

When we decided to write this book and had finished our initial planning, Janis gathered everyone in the office for a book launching. We drank champagne, ate cake, and toasted to the endeavor's success. This came as a surprise to me, but a positive one.

This book was our first experience of working together on a long-term project. We started our partnership with a trip through the Tennessee mountains. Our plan was to travel via automobile to one of Janis' Quality R+ seminars with Tennessee Eastman in Kingsport.

We tape recorded much material for the book on this trip. Along the way, we rewarded ourselves by stopping for treats and cups of coffee when we had covered a set amount of material.

On the return trip we pulled over at a wide space in the road in the middle of the Tennessee mountains. On display, hanging on a clothes wire, were some beautiful handmade quilts.

Janis engaged me in a casual conversation about the color schemes of our respective homes. Then she asked me to help her pick out a quilt for her mother's Christmas gift. I was flattered she would ask my opinion because Janis has a reputation as a savvy decorator.

Of course, I picked the quilt that I found most attractive.

I was completely surprised when, several days later, the quilt arrived, boxed, at my doorstep. I headed for the phone to tell Janis that somehow her mother's quilt had been erroneously shipped to my address. Then, I noticed, pinned to the quilt, a note from Janis telling me how she liked my work.

I was elated. My productivity was effectively cut in half that day. I was too busy calling people, telling them about the quilt, and looking at it. My enthusiasm and confidence about the book instantly elevated (along with my productivity the next day). Janis gave me a quality reinforcer that tells a story and I tell that story to every person when I show off the quilt.

Throughout the production of this book, Janis wrote positive notes and helpful feedback in the margins of the rough drafts. She distributed (to my initial horror) unedited copies to clients and co-workers. She then immediately returned the feedback, all helpful and positive, to me. She sent positive notes on our electronic mail regarding our progress and copied them to others in the company.

Once, while I was in the middle of a long day at the computer keyboard, my doorbell rang. A container painted with Halloween pumpkins and full of popcorn (one of my major weaknesses) sat at the door. The message read, "For great writing, from your co-author." I left a message on Janis' home phone recorder, "If you think all this reinforcement is going to work on me you're totally right."

I must add that Janis had the perfect patient to test her quality reinforcement techniques on — me. I soon realized that over the years I've become an expert at deflecting reinforcement. As Janis candidly and continuously pointed out, "You're doing it again."

I can't claim I'm completely cured of my deflecting ways, but I have learned a great deal about receiving and giving reinforcement. I credit Janis for that. She is truly a quality reinforcer.

ABOUT THE BOOK: JANIS' STORY

The writing trip Gail and I took to Tennessee was a highlight and the keystone to the writing of this book. For me, writing (which was talking, because we recorded the material) was my Premack reinforcer for staying in the car for six hours. It wasn't work, but fun to keep driving on up the road. Also, I enjoy Gail's company. We have many mutual interests and laugh at the same jokes, puns, and word plays.

I enjoyed it when she and I sprawled out on my den floor while working on the first draft. We liked getting out of the office and away from the phones to flesh out the book's beginning. We did quite a bit of writing, and rewarded ourselves with several rounds of Canberry's Diet Cherry Chocolate Fudge Soda.

I especially enjoyed a bag of goodies Gail gave me when I went off for a secluded weekend in the woods to work on the book. In the bag she included a tape recorder (my own to keep) and some blank tapes so I could record my remarks about the book. She also included M&Ms, a book of Far Side cartoons, a bottle of champagne, and a special issue of *Time* magazine, all on my reinforcer list.

She also threw in some items that were private jokes, such as a miniature plastic hamburger and fries. These symbolized our trip to Tennessee when we had created the bulk of our book. We also added to our own bulk by stopping at every fast food restaurant along the way.

We both still relive some of our experiences and the laughs we had on our Tennessee trip. Gail gave me a copy of the best seller, *It Was On Fire When I Lay Down On It* by Robert Fulghum. I had mentioned I would like to use the book's format as a model for our own.

At the end of the writing and editing and rewriting process, nine months after we had begun, it was proof-reading time. Gail and I asked Brenda Jernigan and Sandy Stewart if we could be present for their next-to-last proofing session. They had already read the book once and made some excellent suggestions and raised some important technical issues which we were able to clarify by re-writing.

The four of us planned to get started at 1:00 p.m. on a Tuesday afternoon at my house. Our plan was to set up ratio reinforcement for ourselves; to go out to dinner together at whatever time we finished. We sat rocking on my front porch and savored Atlanta's March breeze, with the dogwoods at their peak.

At 8:00 p.m., we weren't quite to the halfway point, so we dialed "Ring Mr. Ching" to deliver cashew chicken and pork fried rice. By then we were all sitting or lying on the floor in the den. Everyone took whatever time we needed to discuss every questionable item and made the book more consistent, readable, grammatically correct, and visually appealing. We finally finished at 3:45 a.m.

Thinking back to my writing-in-the-woods weekend, after editing the first draft, I had noticed some stickers Gail had stashed in my R+ pack. To reward myself for my diligent efforts that weekend, I took one out, stuck it on the last page, all alone, and said out loud, "I'm finished."

I think I'll do that now.

SUBJECT INDEX

NAME INDEX